Scout Leaders in Action

Scout Leaders in Action

Walter G. MacPeek

Abingdon Press

NASHVILLE AND NEW YORK

SCOUT LEADERS IN ACTION

Copyright © 1969 by Abingdon Press

Standard Book Number: 687-37029-9

Library of Congress Catalog Card Number: 69-18454

The lines on p. 129 from "On moonlit heath and lonesome bank"
from "A Shropshire Lad," Authorized Edition, from *The Collected
Poems of A. E. Housman.* Copyright 1939, 1940, © 1959 by Holt,
Rinehart and Winston, Inc. Copyright © 1967 by Robert E. Symons.
Reprinted by permission of Holt, Rinehart and Winston, Inc. and The
Society of Authors as the literary representative of the Estate of A. E.
Housman, and Messrs. Jonathan Cape Ltd., publishers of A. E. Hous-
man's *Collected Poems.*
The lines on p. 101 from Gerald Gould's "Wander-Thirst" from *The
Collected Poems of Gerald Gould* by permission of Victor Gollancz Ltd.

SET UP, PRINTED, AND BOUND BY THE
PARTHENON PRESS, AT NASHVILLE,
TENNESSEE, UNITED STATES OF AMERICA

Dedicated to

the devoted men and women of yesterday, today, and tomorrow who give of themselves in the enrichment of boy life through their resourcefulness in helping boys to grow into their fullest possible selves

Introduction

There are thousands of incidents about Scout leaders that should be told, incidents that reveal the dedication, ingenuity, and resourcefulness of these many thousands of men and women who help youngsters achieve their full potential. During the past fifty years as a Scout leader, the author of this book, Walter MacPeek, has written down many such incidents in boy life as he has obesrved them or as they have been told to him.

Mr. MacPeek has compiled and edited two previous books, *The Scout Law in Action,* and *The Scout Oath in Action.* These pocket-size volumes have already become essential parts of our library of Scouting literature. They are helping all of us, boys and adults alike, to keep our eyes focused upon the ideals of Scouting.

In this volume intended for adult reading, Walt has gathered this series of interpretations from his own writings, emphasizing the methods, influences, and procedures of scout leaders, past, present, and future.

I commend *Scout Leaders in Action* to you. You will find that it will help you in better understanding and appreciating the far-reaching contribution that has been made and is being made to America by these great-hearted and devoted men and women.

ALDEN G. BARBER
Chief Scout Executive

Foreword

More than fifty years ago in a small town in northwestern Illinois, a man cared enough about a gang of noisy, enthusiastic, adventure-seeking boys to be willing to live with them—my old scoutmaster. He went camping with us, challenged us with the ideals of the scout oath and law, and lived with us in troop meetings, on service projects, and in camp.

Since then I have known, observed, and admired many hundreds of scout leaders and have occasionally written down some of their adventures in living with and in influencing boys.

What have I observed of the influence of these understanding and great-hearted men and women? I have found that their personal influence, the kind of people they are, becomes very significant in the lives of boys. I have found that many of these Scout leaders have an uncanny understanding of what makes a boy tick. I have found them to be encouragers who helped to build up boys rather than find fault with them.

I have observed that they help boys to widen their horizons, to develop skill in living with people, to encourage them to reach high for real values.

They help boys to discover and use their own inner resources, to build upon discipline values, and to gain experience in making wise choices.

Perhaps by now you gather that I think the more than a million adult scout leaders are a pretty vital part of America's fabric of resources. You're right. I do.

If this book, along with its companion volumes, *The Scout Law in Action* and *The Scout Oath in Action*, will encourage you to value highly the far-reaching contribution that these Scout leaders, the great majority of whom are volunteers, are making to America, it will have accomplished its purpose.

WALTER G. MacPEEK
North Brunswick, New Jersey

Contents

Chapter 1

Personal Influence

OF ALL THE THINGS YOU DO, PROBABLY NO ONE
OF THEM—OR ALL COMBINED ARE AS IMPOR-
TANT AS IS YOUR PERSONAL INFLUENCE.

Men and women of widely varying personal qualities and
resources find deep satisfaction in serving as leaders in scouting because they know their influence may be significant.

Den mothers often have far-reaching personal influence in
the lives of the youngsters in their dens. Scoutmasters, directly
and through the impact of other adults, contribute significantly
to the enrichment of boys' lives. Explorer Advisors and other
Scouters exert unmeasurable personal influence on the lives
of boys and young men.

Sympathetic Understanding

We are wise when we do not expect too much of a boy. He
is not born honest, nor industrious, nor with a highly developed
power of creativity. He is like a growing vine reaching out,
or up, or down, according to the trellis work of the life setting

which he finds confronting him. He responds to the climate of values in which he finds himself.

Many people are beginning to study the nature and needs of boys, but there are still more books available on how to play bridge or how to build a house than there are on how to help a boy become his fullest possible self. One phase of sympathetic understanding that a youngster needs as he grows up is the willingness of adults around him to allow him to start where he is and work toward the goal, which we may hope that he will move toward.

The boy's nature is such that he admires action. A boy recently expressed to his mother, after having seen a picture of the Rough Riders, "I'd rather be a Rough Rider than an angel!" Such are liable to be the choices of youth.

Everyday Heroes

Boys need some super-special heroes like Washington, Lincoln, and Roosevelt. But they also need to have some heroes *close to home*. They need to know some men of towering integrity on a face-to-face basis. They need to meet them on the street, to hike and camp with them, to live with them in everyday down-to-earth situations, to feel close enough to them to ask questions and to talk things over with them in a man-to-man fashion. Boys need to learn that great worth, earnest purpose, and high idealism can be motivating forces in the lives of humble but great everyday men, who may be not widely known or publicly acclaimed. Boys need to rub shoulders with men who have genuine pride in honest workmanship, solid integrity, and sense of responsibility—not necessarily famous men but fundamentally good citizens, men who live down the street or just around the corner.

One of the greatest tragedies that can come to any boy is for him to accept the wrong kind of heroes—heroes too small.

Yet there is possibly a still greater tragedy—the disaster to the spirit of a boy who never discovered any heroes at all! Boys need heroes who walk and talk and eat, who go to church, who read books—men who dream of helping in their everyday way to build a better world. There is bravery there and heroism sometimes in the lives of these everyday people who live close by. There has to be, and boys need to know about it.

Men Who Showed the Way

"I never became famous. I'm just an ordinary sort of a fellow," a scoutmaster told me at a Valley Forge Jamboree. Then I saw his shoulders go back just the least bit, and I could detect an extra touch of pride in his voice as he went on, "But one of the boys in my old troop is a college president and another is a full colonel." He had every right to feel proud that some of the boys whom he had helped to show the way had climbed high on the ladder of achievement.

I have seldom talked with an outstanding man who has not paid tribute to some man in his youth who encouraged and inspired him.

Thomas Jefferson said of one of his professors, Dr. William Small, "From his conversations, I got my first views of the expansion of science and the system of things in which we are placed."

James Madison said of George Robertson, his teacher, mentor, and friend, "All that I have been in life I owe largely to that man."

We are all familiar with the frequently advanced idea that a college might consist of Mark Hopkins on one end of a log and a student on the other. History has certainly indicated this to be an unbeatable combination—a wise, great-hearted teacher and an eager boy, hungry for knowledge, eager to learn—each respecting the other.

A book might be compiled listing the men, many of them relatively unheralded, who have greatly influenced boys who have made great contributions to the world.

Perhaps there is no more significant task for a man than this: to help boys discover the way to usefulness, perhaps even to greatness.

More Doing with Instead of Doing For

Let's recognize when we deal with youth that *they* must have a part in the purposing. Almost before a youngster is old enough to walk he says, "Let me do it," and he pushes away grown-ups so that he may have a chance to try his strength and his ingenuity on a task. From then on until he is grown, sometimes vocally, sometimes with a feeling of open or suppressed antagonism or irritability, by word and deed, he pushes adults away saying, "Let me do it!"

Yet we grown-ups constantly attempt to do things *for* him rather than *with* him. *He needs more doing with.*

More of the spirit of friendly teamwork between grown-ups and youngsters is needed. This teamwork, of course, requires a sympathy and a respect for each other. We cannot be impatient; we must not expect perfection. We have to learn, we grown-ups, to look at things again through the eyes of youth and be reasonable in our expectations. We cannot expect young people to move with the speed and with the sureness that adults can.

"Is there another problem?" you may ask. Are young people willing and eager to have grownups work with them? Wouldn't they sooner be left to themselves? Yes, they will accept our help if we can work with patience and understanding.

If we are going to do more things *with* youth, we must achieve skill in working unobtrusively. We must stop expecting to be appreciated for the "sacrifice" we are making. If one is to succeed in working with youth, he must be able to earn his place as a friend and cooperator, fellow discoverer, and adventurer with youth. Some adults do achieve that relationship. More of us *could*.

Slim Huzzer or Bill Wilson

Someone wisely said that scouting experiences provide a chance for the boy in the man to reach out to the man in the boy. Come with me on a journey into boyland and see some of the hopes, dreams, and disappointments that sometimes take place in the heart of a boy as he responds to the influence of the men he meets.

I remember the picturesque figure of Slim Huzzer. He was over six feet tall, broad-shouldered, and big-hearted. He liked boys. He was active, always moving, always doing something. Naturally boys liked him. Unfortunately Slim Huzzer got drunk at regular intervals, made his living by gambling, and punctuated his conversation with cursing. Yet in my little hometown many boys formed their image of manhood from this man.

As years went by and Slim Huzzer took up his residence in one of the institutions of our state, most of the boys of the community found another hero. He, too, was big-hearted. He was ever willing to listen to the problems that comfront and puzzle boys. He was always ready to go on hikes with us and to take part in the rugged, manly activities which boys enjoy. Bill Wilson was a *thorough gentleman*. He owned his small business, and he became the ideal of almost every boy in town.

Boys everywhere need manly leadership. They need association with the strongest and ablest men in any community. It is the duty of all of us to see that it is made easy for boys to follow in the footsteps of strong men along the trail that leads uphill.

In many communities Slim Huzzers seem more readily available than Bill Wilsons, but thoughtful community leaders will find the Bill Wilsons and enlist them to help surround youth with wholesome influences.

Dawn of a New Day in a Scoutmaster's Life

(In eight scenes, suitable for use at a leaders' meeting)

Scene 1: *Scoutmaster is seated talking to himself, yet loud enough to be heard.*

> Oh, what's the use?
>
> Why should I give up my time when parents just don't seem to care? My troop committee is just a bunch of nice-looking names on a piece of paper. They never turn their hand to help me.
>
> I don't see my neighborhood commissioner once in six months.
>
> The boys don't take any responsibility. I think I'll quit. Why should I care if nobody else does? (*He puts his head on the desk and sleeps.*)

Scene 2: *From the left a Scout enters who addresses the sleeping Scoutmaster.*

> Remember me? I'm Bill Jones. I suppose I'm one of those boys that you say won't take any responsi-

bility. You told me one night that I was a patrol leader. I was so excited about it that night that I could hardly sleep.

I tried hard to *be* a patrol leader but I just *didn't know how.* I didn't even know there was a *Patrol Leader's Handbook.* You must remember that whenever we had a patrol leader's meeting to plan together, I *wanted* desperately to help, but you men didn't give me much of a chance. So I dropped out. (*Scoutmaster stirs uneasily.*)

Scene 3: *Enter a man.*

Remember me? Nine years ago I was a Scout in your troop. I was later a marine in the war.

You were a great Scoutmaster. Your friendliness helped me more than I can tell you. The spirit of Scouting has meant a great deal to me. The camping I learned with you has made the difference between my having been a poor soldier or a good one. I'll never cease to be grateful to you.

Scene 4: *Another boy enters.*

Do you remember me—little Whitey? That night you pinned my Tenderfoot badge on me, I promised myself that I would be an Eagle some day. Perhaps I promised you too, but I failed. I stayed in the troop a little over a year, but things got pretty dead, and I finally quit. I'm sorry because I *needed to succeed.* I needed to form the *habit* of succeeding. It's a habit that lasts all through life—people tell me.

Scene 5: *Man enters from left.*

I guess I was pretty much of a fizzle as a troop committeeman, and I won't try to excuse myself. Perhaps I was trying to compliment you by telling myself that I let you alone and let you run the troop.

I would have been glad to help if you had asked me or if the chairman had asked me to do something specific, but I was a little sensitive about pushing myself forward.

You used to be a great Scoutmaster. My boy thinks you're the greatest guy in the world. But the last year or two I've been hearing that the troop is slipping. I'm ready to help again if I can, but having fallen down on the job once, I'd have to be awfully sure that you really *want* me.

Scene 6: *Boy enters from left.*

When you made a list of dropped Scouts you wrote down that I had lost interest. I didn't lose interest at all. I just got fed up with haphazard meetings in the church basement.

I wanted to do Scouting the way it says in the handbook. I wanted to hike and cook and make trails. In the last five months that I was in the troop we didn't have one hike or go to camp. I was just starved to death for some small taste of real Scouting.

Scene 7: *Small boy enters from left.*

I'm Bill Brown. I'm going to be eleven next month. I'm going to join your troop. You know why I'm going to join?

I want to have fun and go on hikes. I want to be in a good patrol. I want to advance in rank. I want to have a lot of friends. I know that it will help me if I have some men to call my friends. Maybe I can get them from among the troop committeemen, merit badge counselors, and leaders in camp. If you let the troop slide, you are going to disappoint us.

My folks will help you. My dad and mother will do almost anything to help the troop I'm in. You just give them a chance and see how willing they are to help the Scoutmaster of our troop.

Scene 8: *Scoutmaster lifts his head. He muses:*

Yes, they all were right—all six of them.

Bill Jones never had a chance to succeed as a manager of his patrol because we men didn't train him.

But Ed found life a bit more bearable in the Marines because of what our troop did for *him.*

Yes, Whitey, we let you down. Somehow we didn't realize how desperately important you were. But I pledge to you and to the other Whitey's still coming along that from now on *we will do our best.*

And troop committeeman Tom—sure we'll put you to work in earnest. We need manpower. You're it.

Bob, I know now that it was our failure that led to your falling down, but never again.

And Bill Brown, half-past ten, almost eleven— eleven years old, I mean—I know that you and your parents, too, will help.

Aside. No, we just don't dare fail. A man *must* do his job or make way for a man who will.

No, this troop must not go down hill. This troop must not drift. We're going ahead!

A Camp Leader for My Son

For many years I've been a staff member or director of various boy's camps. I've seen a lot of counselors and leaders during those years. Most of them have been pretty fine people.

But before long, my own boy will be going to a summer camp. He's our only son—our single contribution to the future of the world. Naturally, we're pretty anxious that his camp experience be a good one.

What are the qualifications that we would like in the young men who are to be his camp leaders as they become so important a part of his world?

First, I'd hope that this camp staff member would take his job seriously—would be *in earnest*. I'd hope that he would recognize the high calling of being a leader in a camp. I'd hope that he wouldn't be a mere popularity seeker—an "anything goes" sort of person.

I'd hope that he would be clean in language and thought. Of course, we sort of expect that unless he has a pretty wholesome and positive outlook he just wouldn't be a leader in camp.

Third, I'd hope that this young man would have a good deal of boyish enthusiasm, and yet with it all have pretty much the standards and values of a grown man. I'd like him to know how to work hard and play hard—at the proper times.

Then I'd hope that he would not be a bully—nor a scold. I'd hope that the influencing of the development and growth of my boy's personality would be a great joy and challenge.

I'd hope that this leader would be a quiet, modest person —not a loud-mouthed, noisy, unsure-of-himself sort.

Yes, I want quite a bit from this camp leader. May I add one more to this already demanding array of attributes? May this prince among people lead my son into new, wholesome curiosities and explorations. I'd hope he would not try to lecture or use other classroom methods. My son has that sort of experience all year round. In camp I hope his leader will help stimulate his curiosity—his eagerness to explore and to learn—to be a fellow discoverer with him.

Yes, these are some of the values I want for my boy more than anything else in the world. Am I expecting too much?

Contagious Citizenship

What a privilege it is for a man or a woman to share in the shaping of the life, purpose, and sense of values of a boy.

You are certainly fortunate among the people of your community to be given this high trust, to be able to work in this sacred task of helping boys grow into good citizens.

It's work—lots of it. It takes patience and understanding and skill. But it's worth it.

Along the Way

I may not have another chance to help that boy. I have this one chance, this one smile, this one word to influence his courage and perhaps to increase his goodwill, and then his path leads on away from mine.

Perhaps in this brief moment I can open a door for him, so that he may better glimpse some value that he did not see before. Or possibly by some friendly, understanding thought I can help him search more deeply and take a firmer grip on life.

I may thus become a useful part of his unfolding life.

A Boy's Gang

A boy must have friends of his own age. He cannot grow up without them. What those friends think is important to him; their standards are often the most important single control in a boy's life at some period in his development.

He is guided to a great degree—whether we like it or not—by the values by which the gang lives. There is not much that we can do about whether or not a boy is going to be influenced by other boys. But there is a great deal we *can* do in encouraging a boy to get into a good gang—a gang that lives constructively, restricting themselves and trying to help other people.

Your church probably has such a gang—called a Boy Scout troop—and would welcome your knowing about and taking pride in it. The leader of that troop is probably a father, maybe like yourself, concerned about his son and about other fathers' sons.

Then you may find, on the other hand, that the fathers in your town think they are "too busy" to do very much about the boys of your community, too busy with other things that will not matter half as much!

If you want your boy and his friends to be in a good gang, surrounded by helpful values, it's a pretty good idea to show your interest and to offer your help. Few things in the world will pay off more.

Man at Work

Instead of bemoaning and complaining about the immaturity of youth, a Scout leader projects boys into situations that will help them become more mature. He knows that criticism of a boy for his weak muscles, or his lack of skill, or his poor judgment, or his feeble courage, helps very little.

He realizes that what the boy needs is practice and more practice.

He likes to see a youngster involved in situations which contribute to the boy's training, his appreciations, and his use of these values in daily life.

The Scout leader rates the training value of an experience as of more value to the boy than the score the boy may make; as he says, "The en route values are often greater than the destination benefits."

The Leader's Influence

A boy needs to have the feeling that people understand him, feel concern for him, respect him, and are fully sympathetic with his efforts to become a man.

"Time and again, when reading case histories of people who have gone wrong, one is struck by the fact that the man's brother or sister in the same family, with the same background, and the same handicaps, turned out all right," Rudolph Wittenberg says in *So You Want to Help People*. "If one does a little digging, he will usually find that the man who turned out well had the good fortune *to find someone who understood him when he needed it most.*"

If a parent, someone in school, a Scout Leader, or other person whom he respects, offers this kind of empathy—and the boy knows it—he is fortunate indeed. Such a friend should be a constant reinforcement, but there are special crisis times when the boy *must* have his assurance.

A Scoutmaster's Response

The boy had probably never had an ax in his hands before. Perhaps he was flustered and awed at the strangeness and bigness of the out-of-doors. He had borrowed his Scoutmaster's ax and proceeded to chop—neglecting to first remove the leather sheath!

What did his greathearted Scoutmaster say? He thought for a moment—thought with his heart. Then calmly he said, "Son, I guess that wasn't much of a sheath anyway, but it's the only one I have."

The Tenderfoot, subdued by his thoughtless action, viewed the chopped sheath and said, "Mr. Clark, if you'll help me, I'll make you a new one, a better one than that was." There's one Dallas Scoutmaster who is pretty proud of his new ax sheath and even more proud of the Scout who made it.

A Scout Leader Makes These Things Happen

• He helps to make rich, strong, worthwhile forces, influences, and experiences happen in the lives of boys—such as good reading, camping adventure, experiences of achievement, and friendly associations with strong men and boys.

• He works with indefinite, intangible forces that he cannot see—the spirit and the *potentials* of boyhood. He harnesses such invisible forces as troop morale and teamwork to help develop character in boys.

• He becomes an expert in human relations—a cooperator with home and church and school, as interested in *their* work as he is in his own. He is the general manager of a corporation of buoyant doers.

• As a personnel director, selecting and training boys to be leaders of other boys, he helps plan a program that has in it that sparkle of adventure and romance that will attract and hold boys in Scouting, under the atmosphere of strong, helpful, positive, influences.

• He keeps the Scout Oath and Law ever before boys as a code of conduct to use in active, everyday life.

• He lists and inspires other men to work with him to give of themselves for boyhood enrichment.

• He keeps things constantly moving, discovering new ways and refreshing old ways of helping boys discover the potential within themselves and bring it into everyday use.

• Then, too, the Scout leader himself must keep growing, ever reaching outward and upward, better preparing himself to be a more competent leader of boy leaders.

Never let any man tell you that a Scout leader is not important. He has a job that is staggering in its importance and its opportunities. It is so far-reaching that it requires a big man who will give his very best.

Leaders of youth, may you be happy and successful in your job of leadership, in your field of influence, for yours is one of the biggest and most important jobs in the world.

Men Wanted!

Scouting needs men who feel and keep close to the needs and yearnings of boys—understanding the complexities of their world, their relationships with parents, their tensions, problems, and satisfactions—men who can thrill to on-moving community life, who can be a little more understanding, a bit more magnanimous, a bit more purposeful than others around them.

Great Opportunity to Be a Counselor and Friend

One of the most important phases of the Scout leader's job is to sit down as frequently as possible and visit with the boys of his troop individually and unhurriedly. Too many Scoutmasters tend to think of their job as "running the troop" or at least being the executive officer of the troop. Important as these administrative responsibilities are, of even greater value *can be* the too often overlooked opportunities of *listening* to boys and talking things through with them.

"When can I find the time?" you ask.

"How about a setup in which boys will come to me to talk things over?" another leader asks.

How about a face-to-face conference in his home or in your home or office with every new boy *before* he joins the troop. Then follow up on these friendly visits every few weeks.

A leader might say, "Bill, could you come over to my house for a few minutes Wednesday night? I'd like to talk over some things with you."

The door is wide open for the troop leader. Of course, the merit badge counselor, too, has a rare opportunity to chat with a boy, to listen to his reactions to school, to his hobbies, to his troop and to his community. The merit badge counselor can often stimulate and guide a boy with new interests and new explorations.

The camp leader has a most strategic opportunity, too, to be a friend and counselor in an atmosphere heightened by the freedom from restraint and in the free and easy setting of life in the open.

Then, too, on some troop committees there is a reading counselor. There is open to him a rich opportunity to be a friend to a boy and to help the boy to broaden his horizon through the discussion of books—and of many other topics.

If I were a Scoutmaster again—and I hope to be one again some day—I would try to spend *at least half* of my available Scouting time in being a friend and counselor to individual boys.

Ask any man who was once a Scout what he remembers most happily from his Scouting days, and often he will say, "Oh, camping trips and getting my life award—but most of all, the *friendships* I made with men—especially with my old Scoutmaster."

Influences That Last

Several young businessmen were reminiscing in front of the fireplace. "Yes, I know, Bill. But why is it that a boy's Scouting experience often so grips him that it becomes the dominating force in his life for many years to come—that is, of course, when he actually gets a real taste of Scouting?"

"I'm pretty sure it's *partly* because of the admiration he has for that fine man who is making the troop possible, his Scoutmaster. I remember as a youngster how I almost worshiped the ground that my Scoutmaster walked on."

"The funny thing about it with me, fellows, is that in my experience the Scoutmaster didn't make as much impression on me as another Scouter did. Mr. Hendry was the chairman of our troop committee, and as Scoutmasters came and went, Mr. Hendry held on year after year. There was something about him, quiet and unassuming, that sort of touched the heart of us kids. He was one of the humblest, most approachable men I ever knew. We knew that he didn't own very much in the way of worldly goods, but we discovered that he was always willing to share whatever he had with us. I'll bet that every fellow who was ever in old Troop 4 is a finer man today because of the respect each of us had for Mr. Hendry. I suppose as chairman of that committee he helped pin the Tenderfoot badge on a couple of hundred boys. Somehow you listen to what a man tells you when he is pinning on that first badge."

Another man spoke up: "I suppose I had an unusual advantage as scribe of our troop—the kind of chance that few other boys had. In my little hometown we had as the secretary-treasurer of our troop committee the man who was truly the town Santa Claus. He was a banker, big hearted to a fault, friendly and kindly, and yet strictly business. Nothing halfway or slipshod would do with him.

"I remember how week after week, very much scared at first, I used to take my scribe's record book to him, and there in his director's room at the bank we would look through the record book together. It would take a great deal of money to get me to give up the memory and the values of the lessons in thoroughness and neatness that I got from him in those years that I served as troop scribe. Then when I finished high school, he helped me get my first job."

"I guess we never thought anything about it at the time, and I never really realized until years later how much it meant, but as I look back over my years in the Scout troop and the limited progress I made, I recall that our school superintendent, Mr. Myers, who was the advancement member of our troop committee, visited our meeting every few weeks. On those occasions, as we jokingly said, 'We ran the gauntlet.'

"I can see him just as clearly now—how he sat at his little table in the corner with his glasses way down near the end of his nose. Our Scoutmaster sent us to him, one by one, to look over the chart which he kept, which showed whether or not we were at work advancing toward our next rank.

"As it worked out, most of us arranged our program so that we could report to him that we had made some advancement since the last time. Of course we were anxious to please our bighearted Scoutmaster, but I'm sure that this extra man, personally interested in us, made it just that much more urgent that we keep right on the job."

"Well, we seem to be singing the praises of the members of the troop committee tonight. Have we left anybody out?"

"Yes, we have—the man who I think can be and often is the most important on the whole troop committee, the man who works closely with the Scoutmaster on the outdoor program. It happened that when I was a kid in a Scout troop, our Scoutmaster had to work every Saturday afternoon and evening, but Mr. Parker, 'Cliff' we called him, was the outdoor man on the troop committee, and, believe me, we had some real hikes and camping trips with him."

"I remember our neighborhood commissioner, too," another suggested. "Over a period of years he was faithful and helpful. Only a few of the boys got to know him well, but we admired and respected him. He was our friend."

And so these men agreed that of those Scouting experiences those looming highest among often recalled and deeply cherished events were the opportunities that came to them to get to know quite a few Scouters related to their troop. The recollections of the influences of those men are among their most cherished memories as they look back on their Scouting days.

Chapter 2

Understanding What Makes a Boy Tick

YOU HAVE TO UNDERSTAND BOYS IN ORDER TO
HELP THEM. MEN AND WOMEN HAVE FOUND THAT
THEIR UNDERSTANDING OF WHAT MAKES A BOY
TICK IS THE POINT OF BEGINNING.

When an adult has begun to develop an understanding, based upon a genuine respect for what the boy is and is becoming, he is well under way.

"Understand the boy" can well be the first item on the job analysis of the man who takes seriously his influence in dealing with youth. It is a progressive relationship, continuous, never fully achieved.

The Tug-of-War Within the Boy

The boy's inner nature demands that he be active and unrestrained—that he run and jump and shout and be free. But on frequent occasions he must learn to control this boisterous activity if he is to grow to be a self-controlled adult.

Over against these demands of his inner nature, urges for action and noisy outlet, are other important demands of home and school and community. All these forces insist that in addition to being a free individual he must learn to become a part of a group—he must become a disciplined teamwork member of society.

Very early in life these two conflicting demands start pulling the boy, often in opposing directions. These pulls continue until he learns to conform.

You are his friend, his guide, a philosopher of boy nature who understands these conflicting urges. You understand the demand of his nature to be wild and free. At the same time you recognize the demand of society for him to be a self-disciplined teamworker in a group.

You have enough patience and understanding to recognize these conflicting demands upon him, but the boy himself is not yet a philosopher. He is often the baffled victim—a relatively simple and uncomplicated person—baffled and bewildered by the buffeting of the complex world in which he finds himself.

Through external compulsion the boy may be forced to comply with rules and regulations. But external force alone cannot call forth his understanding and wholehearted co-operation.

Adherence to a rule can sometimes be forced on a boy from without. But respect for and love of truth and justice and honor can come only from inner growth and desire. Attitudes grow from experiences that have touched something inside him, attitudes which understanding adults—like yourself—have a part in forming.

What the boy is forced to do has much smaller character residue than that experience in which he participates because he wants to, for then his desires and choices and attitudes are aroused.

Redirection of a Tendency

I remember as a youngster on a farm, that a small creek was gradually cutting in under the roadway. In only a few months, unless something had been done, this undercutting would have made the road impassable.

One day I stood watching my father as he contemplated the need for action. I watched with that boylike overestimation of my father's power, with a natural feeling that he could do anything. I suggested that father stop the flow of the creek.

Then, with fatherly patience, he explained to me that the creek could not be stopped but that a channel might be dug which would turn the flow of water to another part of the pasture where it would not only be harmless from the standpoint of damage to the highway, but where it would be useful to provide drinking water for livestock.

Almost every week there comes to each of us the opportunity to redirect a tendency of a boy out of a channel which is unwholesome and harmful; sometimes we have the chance to carry this tendency over into an expression where it will be truly useful. Many tendencies which we cannot stop we can redirect into useful channels.

There is an age at which a boy likes to break things. His destructiveness gets him into difficulties at home and school. To meet this tendency, show him how to use an ax. Get him to chop down a tree. Help him to build something of the logs. You will find him even more eager to use these restless muscles in *building* than in destroying.

Stages

The ears of youth are keen and sharp
And boyhood's memories long.
Our budding son is eight years old,
His love of play is strong.

His mother is most patient,
But often his father's not
So you can see, at times our son
Has not an easy lot.

Sometimes we've grown short-tempered,
Been out of patience grim,
It's true that we have often sighed
For the "next stage" to come to him.

Frequently his parents say,
"He'll soon outgrow this phase."
Sometimes our overeager hopes
Must cloud his boyish, carefree days.

Today, he turned the tables
In innocence of youthful age.
He looked at me, and sighing, said,
"Oh, you'll soon outgrow this stage!"

Patience with a Boy

Why do I try to have patience with a boy as he sometimes stumbles in trying to learn, to observe, to analyze, and to evaluate the conflicting ideas and influences around him? Why do we feel it important that grown-ups help a boy develop a sense of value, even through the baffling process of trial and error?

Why? Because before we know it this eager youngster will be running the works. This is the basis of my feeling toward all boys, but it shows up most forcefully in dealing with boys who show promise of leadership over themselves and over others.

The Process Is Important

Since adolescents are frequently not naturally calm, analytical, deliberative people, since they are instead sometimes inclined to be excitable, enthusiastic, and impatient, and often tend to jump to conclusions, they need to have a great deal of experience *now* in wrestling with problems and in learning to become more efficient in arriving at reasonable decisions. Don't worry about the seeming unimportance of the particular decision. Developing the *process* is the value we are most concerned with.

Bill's Dignity

"I thought you said 'dignity,' " the man interrupted.

"I did. I mentioned the importance of considering the boy's dignity," I explained.

"Oh, but this boy hasn't any such thing. He's noisy and loud and always on the jump. He interrupts you and is flighty and uncontrolled. Maybe his father and his mother have dignity, but not Bill!" my informant declared.

I could see that the other men in the group were pretty much in accord with him. Somehow they hadn't grasped what I was trying to picture.

"Maybe we shouldn't call it dignity, then. Let's call it the sensitive nerve in the boy's reaction, his protectiveness of his sense of importance."

"Nerve is OK with me, like in a toothache! Makes me think of Bill all right," one leader volunteered.

"Does Bill look pretty good at inspection?" I asked.

"Yeah. But you ought to see him two minutes after inspection!"

"How does he react when he is yelled at?" I parried.

"He yells back quite a bit louder."

"That's an indication of his sensitivity, then?"

"Yeah."

"His feelings are hurt enough so that he responds in kind.

Now when you are especially considerate of him, how does he react?" was my next question.

The men looked at each other dubiously. The silence was embarrassing.

"OK," I said, "we won't call it a name, but we do recognize that there's a sensitivity here—a something down inside Bill that makes him respond, either explosively or some other way."

Silence signified more agreement.

"Then our opportunity consists of somehow dealing with this exposed nerve in the toothache situation to bring out the most wholesome possible responses."

"That makes sense," they agreed.

And so we left the matter of Bill's sense of dignity. Perhaps not a very accurate analysis, but at least a beginning.

Traveling up Crandon Hill

Eager faces were reflected by the light from the campfire. A moment before redheaded George Jarvis had asked the Scoutmaster, "Do you think there is danger of going ahead in Scouting too fast?" Immediately following his question there had been a buzz of interest; comments were volunteered from every direction. The Scoutmaster cleared his throat and looked into the fire a moment, silently.

"Can you see Crandon Hill over there in the distance?" he asked, pointing to the hill vaguely silhouetted in the distance. "I have gone up that hill dozens of times. I remember once when traveling in a high-powered car, we rushed up the hillside, hurrying and seeing practically nothing. I remember another time when I was very busy talking to a friend as we drove up the hill, and I was not conscious of any of the beauty along the way. I didn't even see the cedars and the variety of color in the shrubbery and the trees. We were so busy talking that we passed a parked automobile along the road, almost unconscious of it. We found out the next day that a friend of ours had been there, his car broken down, and that he had needed help.

"Then, Scouts, I remembered another time when I went up Crandon Hill. The going was hard, but I was traveling slowly enough that I could see all the beauties along the way. I took my time, and a feeling of happiness welled up in my heart as I saw nature's handiwork all along the way. And then up on a plateau near the top of the hill I caught up with an old man carrying a heavy pack on his back. I gave him a ride. When I let him out down by his shack near the valley, the thankfulness on his face repaid me a hundred times for what little bother I had been to. I like to travel up Crandon Hill slowly enough that I can see, and feel, and help."

"Yes, but how fast do you think a fellow ought to travel toward Eagle rank?" one of the Scouts asked him after a moment's pause.

And the wise Scoutmaster replied, "Figure that out for yourself, but Crandon Hill isn't very much different from the hill that boys sometimes climb in going toward Eagle Scout rank."

"I Was Once a Boy"

"I was once a boy."

With these five words Baden-Powell began the foreword to *Scouting for Boys* in 1908. In the more than fifty years since then the book has had a far-reaching influence in every part of the world, an influence such as few books have had.

Those five words "I was once a boy," stated as his introduction of himself to the reader, reveal some of the kindly understanding of the man. And even more significant, through all the pages of the book he kept that fact clearly in the reader's mind. He never forgot how it feels to be a boy.

As leaders of boys, or as administrators with deep concern for the welfare of boys, it is fundamental that we always keep the needs of the boy foremost in our thinking. We must never let machinery and techniques become so important that we lose sight of the boy's personal welfare for a single moment. Whatever else we do, we must keep our eye on helping the boy.

It is not a bad idea to remind ourselves every once in a while by saying, "I was once a boy."

Discovering Gordon

"Yeah—it's a great theory. But I don't believe it's practical. Most boys may have some fineness of expression, some delicacy hidden way down in their heart, even some tenderness, but this kid is nothing but a rough-and-tumble reckless roughneck. If he has any of what you call 'heart expression,' I don't know how he'd show it. He couldn't sit still long enough. That's Gordon Long."

"Let's talk it over with him. We may make some discoveries."

A few hours later the boy was seated before the two men. "What do you like to do, Gordon?" they had asked him. His noncommittal answers had not been especially significant.

Finally the older man asked him, "Do you like music?"

"Naw—" the boy paused, "not this highbrow stuff."

But the man before him had caught a glimpse of something. He had seen a gleam of light.

"You don't like highbrow stuff, Gordon, but you rather like to hear music that has a happy swing to it, don't you?"

The boy's face lit up.

"Yes—and I can play a cornet—a little."

The men impulsively exchanged quick glances.

"Gordon, I'd like to hear you play. Will your bring your cornet with you sometime?"

"I'll get it now—" and the lad was gone.

"That boy!" the younger man exclaimed. "You must be right. I guess there is some gentleness and tenderness and fineness in every boy's heart. Certainly if there's room for music in that roughneck's soul, I guess you're right."

And somehow Gordon Long's happy, eager smile had a new meaning from then on.

The Boy Is the Starting Point

A Scoutmaster was remonstrating with his troop committee one evening when they had suggested certain possibilities of improvement in the troop. He asked, "What can I do? I can't preach to them, can I?"

He received a response from a discerning committeeman who said, "Sure, you can preach to them, but it probably wouldn't do much good! If we are to be effective, however, we will have to find some other way of getting under their hides."

What he really meant was that we must find a common ground where the interests and the ambitions of the men and the boys meet. We cannot travel along the trail together unless we start from a common point.

You have heard the story of the man in Washington, D. C., who was asked the way to reach the White House. He explained, "Go two blocks to your left, three blocks to your right, one block to your left," and finally in desperation admitted, "Well, if I were going to the White House, I wouldn't start from here."

Too many of us in the guidance of youth lose our temper and our patience and in effect say to boys, "Well, if I were heading for manhood I wouldn't start from where you are!" Yet that is where the boy must start from. That is the point from which we must help him—*if we are to help him at all.*

Dealing with a Boy

I know from experience how a leader of boys feels when a youngster says or does something which viewed by adult standards seems insolent or arrogant. You feel as if a good friend had suddenly thrown a pail of icewater in your face. You feel that this boy, whom you have helped, to whom you've shown patient friendliness beyond the call of duty, has suddenly pulled the rug from under you.

Your first impulse is quite naturally to put the boy in his place, perhaps chew him out—possibly meet temper with temper.

You are fully justified in feeling angry, of course. Yet showing anger will work sadly against accomplishing your long-range goal, which is to help this boy grow to be a man of character, a good citizen.

This overgrown boy of fifteen, so promising at times and overbearing and thoughtless at other times, needs to be brought to see and to regret his unwise action. How can we do this?

Above all else we must handle the emergency calmly. No heated words. No tempers flaring. No voices raised. No vocabularies out of control. Yet this situation is too serious to be overlooked. It calls for a man-to-man talking over.

Often we can handle it better at a later time when his temper, and possibly yours, has cooled. Sometimes he will be sensitive enough to sense your feeling of hurt. Some leaders try using a silent treatment until the boy comes to himself. At other times a leader may give such a boy fewer responsibilities until he has taken steps to right the situation.

Certainly if the offense is serious enough to be disturbing, it needs to be faced. The boy needs to realize that he has done wrong and to feel sorry that he has overstepped. But he should not be put on the defensive. He must not get the idea that he is on one side and that you are against him on the other side. You need to be recognized as standing for the boy, doing everything possible to help him grow to be a man. That is your primary purpose in working with him.

You are not angry at the boy. You are disturbed and disappointed at his demonstrations of arrogance, selfishness, and lack of consideration, but you are not angry at him personally.

Naturally, at the moment you may feel hurt or offended, even tempted to strike back when such an offense occurs. But such action would be likely to defeat your long-range objective of dealing with this boy.

As you think the situation through, you will say to yourself, "This is an opportunity, an unpleasant opportunity, to be sure. Yet, I'll keep cool and impersonal about it. I'll treat the infection, not condemn the patient. His action is not personal toward me. This is a natural awkward emotional outburst of an overgrown adolescent trying desperately to lash out, to become a man. I'm going to be thoughtful and patient in trying to help him."

Is this quite a bit to ask? It certainly is!

And yet if you do not care deeply enough to approach the adolescent boy with something of this long-range attitude of understanding and forgiveness, you are not likely to travel far along the trail with him.

Such problems of human relations are too often handled by violent decision. Then each goes his way—alone.

Thus you have lost your chance to deal wisely and constructively with an unpleasant but significant opportunity. You have failed in your long-range objective, and you have lessened your chance to live in the life of this boy tomorrow.

Counterfeit or Real

"That boy's underlying difficulty is his own feeling of insignificance. He doesn't feel that he is important to himself or to anyone. That's why he's always in people's hair, striving for attention," the learned professor analyzed.

"You've sized Bob up to a 'T,'" I said, "but what is our move? We like Bob. We want to help him, but we're stymied by the way he acts."

"Let's try," the professor suggested, "to give him something real to be admired for. Then he won't have to try to attract attention in that foolish show-off way."

"I begin to see," I said slowly. And so we worked with Bob. We ignored, as best as we could, his occasional outbursts of being unbearable. We knew that he did not believe his own boasting; he was just trying to feed his own sense of adequacy —just playing to the crowd. But whenever Bob did a decent thing, we praised him all we could. We never overlooked a bet to honor him when we could do it in fairness.

Even now months later, Bob is still a good deal of a problem fairly often. But he's beginning to see that our real respect for honest accomplishment on his part gives him much more geniuine satisfaction than the superficial attention he used to pester people into giving him for his misconduct.

Thanks, Professor. We're happier now. And so is Bob.

Youth Rebuilds

Each one of us needs to have an awareness of his own usefulness. We must not, however, confuse this with an exaggerated sense of our own importance. An eagerness to be useful is far different from a desire to seem important. The attitude of the one is an eager questioning, "Can I help you?" and of the other a domineering command, "Salute me. I am good."

A young man gropes along the trail, gradually trying to extend his youthful world into a grown-up man's world. During this process of rebuilding he needs the most sympathetic and kindly guidance possible. Often he is likely to flare up and say exactly what he does not mean to say. At times even his hands and feet seem unable to follow his directions. Sometimes his entire boy's world is wrecked before he has been able to lay out the blueprints or to build even the foundation of the man's world into which he must forge.

Often he seems difficult and unappreciative, discourteous and trying. Yet those of us who in our hearts have the great hope that he will soon be facing the world as a purposeful, powerful man must have patience in our hearts and understanding in our souls as we do what we can in guiding him. He is in the tempestuous years of reconstruction. He is building his boy's world into a man's world.

Youth Does Not Want Soft Ease

Boys have convinced me that the usual idea of many people that boys want ease and desire to have everything done for them is a great fallacy. Boys not only want, but their very nature *demands* that their fiber be made strong, that they be placed face-to-face with situations which are not easy, that opportunities must come to them in which they face the wind and learn not to whine.

Somehow when the world needs a great man, he comes up from the rugged group. We find he is a man whom nature has roughhewn. He is a man who has not had things easy and soft but has had experience in facing and coming through difficult hardening experiences.

Does this sort of challenging life appeal to young people? Read some of the stories of Dr. Grenfell at Labrador and reflect that he had but to lift his finger and dozens of the finest youth of America rushed for a chance to have a part in that project of hardship and service in the far North, far from a life of soft ease.

A King at Heart

"All that Shakespeare says of the king, yonder slip of a boy that reads in the corner feels to be true of himself," Emerson wrote in his essay "History."

Now a prosaic-minded modern might say, "There isn't much market for a king these days. The present supply of kings is entirely adequate."

Perhaps so, and yet, what greater impress can you make in a boy's life than to help him, for a few brief hours at least, to *feel* like a king. He needs to feel the exhilaration and the magnanimity of being kindly in his interest in and love for others.

Boyhood is one of the rare times in life when he will have a chance to feel like a king!

What Makes Boys Behave as They Do

The most fundamental bit of boy psychology that I have discovered has been, "Look back on the particular act of the boy and find the reason for his misbehavior. You will usually find a reason, a cause. Removing this cause is fundamental. Merely removing a symptom or a result of that cause is ineffective, merely working in the dark."

A mother once asked, "How can I keep my boy still?"

"What makes him move?" I asked.

She answered that she had never thought of that.

Part of the trouble that boys face is truly not their trouble at all, but rather the fault of grown-ups expecting a certain kind of activity from them which is not natural to them.

When a boy is active, physically and mentally, he is well. When he runs, jumps, reads, and dreams, he is in a natural state, for these are normal boy activities. Ask a boy to be good and to keep quiet, and you speak in contradiction. It is more logical and by far more natural to ask him to be good and to keep moving.

The trouble with too many of us is that we try to start with the boy at the point at which *we* want him to be rather than starting where he is. We need to encourage him to move in the direction and toward the goal we want for him.

When we start at a point in the boy's world and move toward that world of manhood we want the boy to head for, we work with understanding.

Chapter 3

Encouraging and Building Up Boys

TOO MANY ADULTS ARE INCLINED TO WHITTLE DOWN BOYS, TO BELITTLE THEM, TO IGNORE THEM, AND TO PULL THE RUG FROM UNDER THEM.

Scout leaders help to build up boys, help them to find new strength. And every day they grow more skilled in encouraging and building up boys.

On every possible occasion a boy needs reinforcement, the self-confidence and self-esteem that come from being recognized and treated as a person of worth. That man who helps to encourage and build up a boy, who helps him to discover new strength, both within himself and outside of himself, is rendering a service to that boy, the value of which can hardly be estimated.

Influencing Boys

Keep your mind on the boy he ought to become, and may become—with your help.

If a boy must make a mistake, try to be sure that he learns from it and that it does not put him and you in opposing camps, does not become a catastrophe for him, and does not carry with it a loss of self-respect.

Even though he has made a mistake, even though you cannot approve what he has done, be sure that he understands that he still has your love and respect and willingness to work with him.

Boys Develop Most

- When they want to know. The inner motivation of earnest desire for understanding is a strong one.
- When they feel at ease, yet with a sense of expectancy.
- When they have clear goals.
- When they are at ease with the people in charge.
- When they help to plan ahead.

Encourage and Build Up Boys

Men have found that the basis of success in influencing a boy lies in respecting him. You have to believe in him and in his possibilities so much that you convey that idea of confidence and respect to him as you use patience and skill and understanding in dealing with him. Sure, it takes faith, too.

The editor of a national publication, recalling his old Scout leader of many years ago, said, "Whenever I came to his desk, he either asked me to have a seat or he stood up to talk to me. By this single courtesy he showed that he respected me. He treated me as an equal, as a person important enough to be shown attention. I'll never forget the way that show of respect built me up."

Expectancy

"The Secret of education," Emerson said, "lies in respecting the pupil."

Stated in our own words, slanted toward Scouting, we can suggest that the secret of effective Scoutmastership lies in respecting the Scout and his potentialities, in *re*specting him and in *ex*pecting a great deal from him.

The effective Scoutmaster often needs to try hard to perceive even a faint glimmer of promise. He helps nurture that tiny promise as it grows haltingly into strong purpose through successful performance.

Many times, when a boy has stood at a crossroads where he has had to choose one of many forks in the road, the expectancy of his Scoutmaster, always showing his confidence and belief in the boy, has made the difference.

Don't Be a Belittler

One of the worst ways to spend your time is to let yourself become a "belittler" or a complainer.

Yesterday I heard well-meaning people use such phrases as these: "Oh, he's an idealist," or "He's an eager beaver," or "He's a do-gooder."

The belittler does not detract very much from those whom he calls such names, but he does give a rather good idea of his own sense of values and thinking processes.

The Way We Learn

As I was chatting with a prospective Scout not long ago, he asked me, "Shall I learn the Scout Law by *heart*?"

Somehow the phrase struck me. It may have been something in his boyish tone, something in the pondering way he said "learn the Scout Law by heart."

"Yes," I told him, "with *all* your heart." He looked at me seriously and nodded with comprehension.

There are some things we learn with our heads, maybe

knowledge about camping and firebuilding and identification of trees. But the points of the Scout Law, to use Jimmy's words, we learn with our *heart*, coming to feel them and to understand them more fully the longer and the deeper we live. Think it over, with your heart.

Feeling Pride in Work

Help a boy to feel pride in his work. Help him to feel the thrill of accomplishment when he has performed a difficult task well. Whether he is building a bird-feeding platform, making an Indian headdress or a fire-by-friction set, whatever the task, it is important that he put his very best into his planning and workmanship.

When he is finished with the project, he can then survey it with honest pride, realizing that he has given his *best* to it.

Strategy in Dealing with a Boy

"There are many situations in which you can't get the results you want just by plain brute strength—in dealing with boys, for instance.

"In plumbing work I find that in order to move a heavy piece of equipment, we often have to resort to strategy. We must secure a foothold in order to get power enough to lift a heavy object," Scoutmaster Pete Scott observed. Scott is the wood-badge trained Scoutmaster of Troop 117, Peter E. Howell School P.T.A. of Tucson, Arizona.

"Can you give us a 'for instance'?" I asked the friendly Scouter with the crew-cut graying hair.

"Well, as a Scoutmaster, suppose I think a Scout needs to work more on advancement. Instead of just *urging* advancement point blank, I size him up first, find out all I can about him.

"I discover that he has been pretty much neglected all his life. No one pays much attention to him. He doesn't feel very important. That gives me my contact point. I can help him to feel more useful and important by the way I deal with him. I can pay attention to him, be attentive to what he says. When he does something well, I can notice it and commend him for it."

"That sounds simple," I agreed.

"It is. It's so simple that we often fail to put the idea to use. Start with the boy, his interests, and his needs, and you are using strategy; of course a boy isn't always conscious of the things he'd really like to do."

"Such as what?"

"I was invited not long ago to give a Scouting talk. I figured that the best results would come from the audience hearing directly from a boy. So I picked a boy who would benefit from the experience. At the meeting I took about five minutes to set the stage for him, to introduce him. He then talked for twelve to fourteen minutes and really did a good job.

"He was a bit afraid of the idea at first, but since I was there with him and this was something we had worked on together in advance, he went through with it.

"Now there's one more thing he isn't afraid of and won't be afraid of again as long as he lives. See how much more effective that kind of an experience is than a pep talk on self-confidence could possibly have been?"

Natural Consequences—Cause and Effect

One of the most important services we can perform for any boy is to help him discover the natural consequences of an act.

We can help him see that when a piece of steak is exposed to a flame the fire will smoke it and scorch it. It is a plain case of cause and effect; no favorites, no exceptions, nothing personal about it.

We can help the boy see that the fellow who acts selfishly and thinks only of himself is unpopular and not in good standing with his group. We can help the boy see that carelessness and the losses that come from carelessness are not matters of grudge, nor of someone picking on him, but that these results are natural consequences, merely the result of some action over which he often has full control.

Faulty Method

He was more than devoted to growing youth;
No task was too great, no standard but truth.

Yet his hours of effort seemed in vain;
Through honest eyes he saw small gain.

He studied his plight, he began to review;
Had his plans been faulty, his bases untrue?

Then like a thunderbolt late one night,
The truth came clear, a dawning light.

He's been trying hard, but unwisely no doubt,
To pour goodness in instead of *drawing it out*.

Remnants of a Dream

Many men remember their Scouting days with lumps in their throats—boyhood memories of long-ago days. They thrill to recount over and over again the incidents that bring to mind Scouting's meaning for them—food shared around a campfire, remnants of a dream glimpsed in leaping flames, the handclasp of a good friend who believes in you and helps you to believe in yourself.

Often they recall some man who showed a special interest in that boy long ago; they recall a man who went the extra mile to understand, to counsel, to loan a book, or to reveal and share something of himself to a groping boy.

"He helped me catch some of the meanings of life. He gave me new courage, and he helped me to hold on in Scouting. Without his influence I'm sure I would have tossed in the sponge long before I reached Eagle," one boy says.

The man's name doesn't matter. He is but a symbol of many thousands of devoted, dedicated men who have written their biographies in the lives of boys.

A Successful Scoutmaster

What is there about the way a Scoutmaster does his work that attracts boys and men to his troop? What are the attitudes that help him get results year after year?

He has a sense of responsibility about his job. He isn't one of these "don't care" people we sometimes meet. You never see him shrugging his shoulders and saying, "That's not my job." He gets other people to help—committeemen, boy leaders, and parents. He has a strong sense of responsibility to see that the job gets done. He is determined to see that desirable resources are used and that basic values actually get across in the lives of boys.

Process

There was once a very primitive method of teaching a boy to swim, which consisted chiefly of throwing him in the water and telling him he must sink or swim. Sometimes the results were good—in many cases they were far from satisfactory.

A wise instructor today follows a much different course. The boy is prepared for the experience well in advance. He learns fundamentals of breathing, and his fear is dispersed before he even sees the water. Finally when he is in the water, he is given guidance and help in mastering his stroke and in coordinating his breathing. Naturally this procedure is more satisfactory.

Too frequently we set up many situations in a boy's life and then throw him into a crisis with a sort of sink-or-swim attitude. Can't we learn from the swimming instructor who prepares a boy to meet an emergency before an emergency arises? We can stay with the learner and guide him as he goes through the process. Maybe we can help boys to learn habits of conduct as they acquire swim skills!

Objectives for Scout Leaders

There is little accomplished by merely classifying a boy. If one is to be worthy of the name "leader," he must lead the boy somewhere.

What are some of the common areas of difficulty in a boy's life? This question might well be a starting point for our thinking.

1. One common difficulty is a feeling of *insignificance* or *lack of confidence* in his own importance. Often the boy who has this basic feeling, built up through years of being overlooked, ignored, and held down, tries to give an impression that is just the opposite of this feeling of lack of confidence in his outward, "defense" actions.

Frequently he adopts a "show-off" attitude to try to prove to himself and to others that he does not feel inadequate. The boy who comes into the troop and fails to advance for months, or for years, when he finally drops away from the troop, is often still open to the conviction that he does amount to something, that he can do things, that there is a great spark within him. Scouting's advancement program with its challenges to learn new things, to gain new skills, to experience new situations which he can meet successfully, often is a most valuable tool in helping such a boy build for himself a sense of adequacy. The boy who throws his heart into meeting a situation at thirteen, carried forward with a modest sense of confidence in himself, finds himself years later capable of meeting the problems of thirty years of age.

2. Shall he have a feeling of courage or a feeling of fear? Fear is talked about on every hand. In newspapers and on the radio and in the movies he learns of catastrophies on land and water and in the air. Is it any wonder then that he may be afraid of the dark, of a snake, or of overworking himself? The boy has grown up on a diet too often more heavily tinctured with fear than with courage. Ordinary prudence and common sense are necessary, of course, but that boy who is burdened with a nervous fear that he may drown or break his leg or that some other awful accident may befall him is more likely to undergo such catastrophies than the boy who with equal caution also has an accompanying sense of courage.

Knowledge of how to swim is much better equipment than dread and fear of the water. Certainly the Scoutmaster has an opportunity here to help a boy feel that he is able to master fire and water and danger rather than let them master him. Courage and common sense make a better team than fear and worry.

3. A boy needs a sense of individuality. His Scouting years are not too early for a boy to begin feeling there is work

somewhere that he can do better than anyone else in the world. He has a divine spark within him. He must be challenged with the possibility of realizing his own best self.

Too often boys have a feeling that they are different from other people, difference that in their thinking means inferiority. Often they build defense mechanisms to prove they are like other people. The result is unfortunate. An individual should realize that he is different. Upon that difference often hangs his chance to be greatly useful.

4. A boy needs to learn to know himself. There can be no more far-reaching way in which a Scout leader can contribute to a boy's "finding himself" and finding his place in the world than through friendly counsel and guidance as the boy seeks to discover his own powers, abilities, weaknesses, and interests. As the Scout proceeds from rank to rank, as he adjusts to the intimate relationships within his patrol, as he becomes a good citizen in the troop, participating in community service, in camping projects, and in other ways, this boy learns to know himself and to become conscious of himself as a personality.

A dedicated Scoutmaster has many challenges facing him. None of them can be greater than the challenge to live with youth in such a way as to help them discover a sense of adequacy and usefulness, a feeling of courage, and an appreciation of their own individuality and power.

Scouting Methods

When a boy comes into Scouting, he comes face-to-face with the opportunity of "Scouting" for new knowledge. In some troops the boy is put in the corner and in a parrot-like fashion, and there the knowledge which he needs to learn is poured out to him.

This method may have its values, but it does not develop in the boy the ability to scout for new knowledge, the ability to search and hunt and adventure into new worlds for understanding.

A boy came to his Scoutmaster and asked him, "Mr. Jones, just what kind of leaf is this?" Scoutmaster Jones, on the verge of reply, caught himself and said, "Let's look it up together in your handbook." There ensued a few minutes in which John got a taste of actual practice in using his handbook in a way which would enable him to meet the next scouting-for-information situation that would arise in his life.

Success as a Scoutmaster is determined not so much by what we teach a boy, but by the way we encourage that boy to teach himself, to learn for himself. There are far too many situations in which a leader does something *for* a boy, but not enough mutual *Scouting-together* occasions leading into new worlds and new fields.

The relationship of the Scoutmaster to the patrol leader with whom he is working should be one of co-adventurer, not one who has already adventured and is handing down to his listener a secondhand experience. What you give a boy is of much less value than that which you *help* him *dig out for himself.* That is what is going to count twenty years from now.

We have a responsibility to the boys of continually providing them with the challenge and the opportunity to "scout," to search for new ideas, to "scout" for character and adventure, and to "scout" for real satisfaction. We need to think of these words "scout" and "scouting" as *verbs,* not merely as nouns.

How a Boy Feels About Things

Every once in a while some parent says, "I am surprised at how the Scouting experience has affected my son. He seems to feel so deeply about things."

In a Scout troop a boy is encouraged to care about *values.* His "good turn" is based on his concern for other people. The points of his Scout Law help him to look at the world about him from the point of view of how his actions affect other people.

For instance, consider how a boy feels toward his country. He is taught to treat the flag with respect. Even as a Cub Scout he learned to fold the flag with loving care. He never lets the flag touch the ground. But Scouting tries to go further than merely to teach respect for symbol of our country, as an idea. The boy is encouraged to look behind the symbol. Every good turn emphasizes good citizenship. Whenever a Scout helps his community he is helping America. He is challenged to live for his country, to try to help make it a better nation. This concern is emphasized in his patrol and troop.

At camp he is a citizen in the camp world in which he lives, a situation in which he learns to give and take for the good of the group.

"Every time you are a good citizen you help to strengthen your country," says the *Boy Scout Handbook.*

There are many values Scout leaders try to provide for boys through their everyday Scouting experiences. Leaders especially pinpoint as a part of Scouting's citizenship the value of such qualities as physical fitness. The boy needs to achieve good health and a sound, vigorous body in order to attain his greatest happiness and be prepared to make his contribution to the world in which he lives.

Also, the value of self-reliance is often stressed. The boy needs to learn to depend on his own good judgment. He needs to feel a sense of sureness in his own consciously chosen standards.

Fulfillment of his obligation to God is another important point of emphasis. The boy needs to dedicate and reinforce himself, earnest in his desire to work and to live in harmony with his Creator. He needs to feel and to practice his obligation to God in his everyday living.

The Scout needs encouragement to have experience with and to build a sense of personal responsibility. As he grows, he develops a sense of responsibility for his own growth and development. He sets goals for himself and works toward reaching them.

He needs to be motivated toward being helpful. A boy develops a spirit of service and skillfulness in helping people around him as a natural expression of good citizenship.

He needs to develop a willingness to share. Through association with wise leaders and wholesome associates, the boy finds deep satisfaction in helping and sharing.

He needs to have numerous experiences in democratic living. He learns to understand the democratic processes of government and their values through living and practicing them.

These are some challenges which help to provide opportunities so that in the years ahead Scout-trained men may be well prepared to meet life at their best.

Surmounting Obstacles Is Good Exercise

When things come to people too easily, they grow weak. When young people do not find it necessary to exert themselves, they grow soft, and softness is a sign of weakness.

Abraham Lincoln did not grow soft. He had hard tasks to perform. He had difficulties and obstacles to overcome.

"If you didn't have things quite so easy, son, you'd be a

great deal more of a man someday," might be said truthfully to many boys today.

I find boys every day who will never amount to as much as their fathers do because today they are having things too easy. Everything has been done for them. Overcoming hardships would make men out of them.

Often, overindulgent, well-meaning parents are hothousing and pampering their sons at the awful cost of sacrificing the chance for those boys to become men of power. Strong men do not make soft, easy, lazy choices. To the boy of today we might say, choose hard, rough, rugged, man-building activities. Go on hiking and camping trips. Work hard and play hard. Live strong and clean. Then someday you'll be a man, not because you've dodged obstacles, but because you've developed strong muscles licking them!

Chapter 4

Helping Boys
Widen Their World

A BOY'S WORLD MUST GROW. IF HE DOES NOT
EXPAND HIS WORLD, WIDEN HIS HORIZONS, AND
REACH OUT FOR NEW UNDERSTANDINGS AND RE-
LATIONSHIPS, HE WILL LIVE OUT HIS EXISTENCE
IN A SMALL, COLORLESS, AND DISCOURAGING
CORNER OF THE EARTH, NO MATTER WHERE HE
MAY BE.

A boy needs help in building his world larger. He must
not only live in a large world; he must relate himself to, be
sensitive to, and be conscious of the many-faceted world of
which he is a part. He must be alive and alert to the influences
around him.

Highest Values from Experiences

Start where the boy is; then help him move toward the goal
that beckons to him. Achieving that goal must begin in the
area of the boy's own interests.

Helping a boy to see the natural consequences of an act is
true education. A difficult boy to lead is one who knows too
much that isn't true, who is headstrong without understanding the elements involved in his actions.

Many boys go through a so-called discipline experience having learned the *wrong* lesson.

We must beware of fallacy in punishments. Many men come out of penitentiaries not penitent and through reformatories without any reform having taken place.

There is an obedience still higher than technical obedience to a direct order.

We must be careful that possibilities of higher learnings are not lost. We must not let the especially eager be held back because of the slowness of the majority.

Reassurance

Bob had been having trouble in his patrol, and I had called him to talk things over. Of course he expected a "bawling out."

"One trouble with you, Bob, is that you don't realize what a swell guy you really are," I opened as the boy sat across the desk eyeing me with suspicion.

"Who—me?" he asked, startled that I had something good to say of him. His voice had been argumentative and his attitude belligerent. Now he was genuinely ready to listen, if I had something complimentary to say to him.

Very calmly I pointed out several of the good qualities. I recalled specific times when his actions had been commendable.

"Well, then, you don't think I'm all bad?" he asked, waiting to make sure that he was hearing me correctly.

I reassured him, and the crisis was averted. Our friendship had a firmer basis now.

Discovering Together

A Scout's eyes sparkled as he told me, "I was with my Scoutmaster when we found the fox."

This is the very essence of the Scout program—learning

to discover together. If the man alone had found the fox and merely told the boy about it, the result would not have been the same.

Scouting is a "sharing," not a pouring into. Through Scouting we search for and discover together. We search for life, for abundant faith, for high vision, and for strengthened purpose. That is the basic program of patrol and troop and hike and camp—the basic purpose of the Scout leader.

Inquiring Attitude

An investigative, inquiring attitude is a natural part of the valuable equipment of growing up. Boys take clocks apart to find the tick; little girls remove the doll's head to find out what's inside.

This inquisitive, open-minded curiosity of children can be an appropriate resource for parents and leaders of youth to build on. We can help children discover cause and effect. We can lead them to become scientists on a very simple plane. We can encourage them to take part in an honest and earnest search for truth. Angelo Patri once said, "Even little children can be taught to look at a thing they have done in the light of investigation. They can be taught to look at it without a trace of selfishness that entered into the doing of it. It takes a little longer than the old way, but it works better and lasts longer."

After all, a scientific attitude is a thinking attitude. a questioning, a searching, and leads to discovering the reason for things. Why shouldn't children be given guidance in discovery? What better place than on a hike or camping trip? We must be ever cautious that we help keep the learner's curiosity growing. We must not stifle his search for new knowledge.

Our task is to guide the boy's searching—but to help *stimulate* his *desire to know*.

The boy must desire the food. Educators agree that results are pretty small when we try to force a boy to learn something he does not desire to learn. The first element of education is to *create a desire*. When an eagerness to learn has been established, the learning becomes easier. Scouting education operates on the basis that the boy is first made hungry before he is fed. We first create desire for achievement and accomplishment.

We must arouse desire to know, *to find out*. One of the most difficult feats we face is to make a concept clear to one opposed to seeing it, or to one who has little interest or concern about the matter. If our teaching is to be effective, before it starts we must stir the boy's interest, arouse his wondering, build up his desire for this knowledge and for the accompanying understanding.

Happy eagerness is a part of the learning process. A basic bit of Scouting philosophy is that learning, to be most effective, must be a happy process. At no time should there be an attitude of coercion, of forcing, or of cramming.

Participation in an experience is the genuine process of Scouting education. The boy signals, cooks, hikes, makes maps, ties knots, and builds boats. As he participates in these happy activities, incidentally, almost automatically, for him, he learns certain values. He learns values because he participates in the highest type of happy Scouting learning. Usually he does not participate merely to learn values. He takes part because he enjoys the experience.

Living together and taking part in activities and having experiences are for him the real thing. Gaining skill, mastery, and achievement are incidental results, but important.

The appetite to learn is whetted. In Scouting we try to

avoid artificial stimulants. Someone has described a stimulant as a whip. Most Scout leaders do not consider it wise to cram food down a boy's throat, although they may display "food" rather prominently so there may grow up within the boy a desire to *reach out* for it. But the plan of forced learning has no place in the Scouting procedure.

Sound Education

Get a boy to *want* to know a particular bit of information, and the task of his mastering it is already half accomplished. Purpose is the greatest self-impelling power toward growth.

Create conditions under which a boy will actively seek knowledge, be eager to become competent in a particular field, be eager to gain a special skill, and you have brought about the beginning of the learning process in its most forceful and positive form.

Mastery of knowledge or skill comes quickly when there is a wholehearted desire and determination to make the project work.

The Scouting setting with its challenge and its adventure releases a powerful force within the boy—an eagerness to know—which power goes far toward making his self-development and growth a natural and almost incidental process.

The boy's horizon widens, his understanding grows, almost without his being conscious that fundamental changes are taking place in his life.

Helping Boys Learn

When we deal with people, we need to let them share in the purposing and the planning. This is especially important when we are dealing with youngsters.

People tend to tighten up inside when we become obvious

in doing for them. But they often relax a bit when we ask them to help do something for other people. They will usually really go to town if we first help them to see the need and to feel some concern; then we help them to work out a plan. We work with them moving toward the solution. They delight in sharing in the common task of helping people.

Even before a youngster is old enough to go to school, he begins to say, "Let me do it." He tries to push grown-ups aside, out of his way, while he uses his own ingenuity and strength in accomplishing the task at hand. We grown-ups far too often try to do things *for* youngsters rather than *with* them.

On those rare occasions when we work *with* a young man, far too often we want to do the task in *our* way, not taking time to understand his approach, perhaps even pushing his way aside.

"Well, we are more skilled," you say? Maybe, in some things, but we are concerned with helping him to grow—with helping him to learn how. That is a skill in which he is more proficient than we can be.

He does not learn much through lectures, and he does not learn much through mere watching. He learns most by *doing*, by getting the "feel" of the task at hand, by coming to grips with the situation. Grown-ups need to be big enough to learn to "hold back," to draw a response from the boy with a question or a suggestion instead of squelching his interest by a dictated solution, all wrapped up and tied in a package. Grown-ups need to be big enough and understanding enough to see that the important consideration is that the boy shall grow in skill, in his own performance, and in observing and evaluating, in analyzing, and in searching, while we adults merely guide and encourage this growth on his part.

We help to set up situations; the learner does the finding out. Most of the time *he* needs to lead. We need to *wonder* with him and ask "Would this help?" or "Perhaps we might look here or there."

But the purposing, the trial and error, the weighing, the testing, and the thrill and joy of *creating* and *finding* needs to be mostly the boy's own.

What a Boy Cares About

What a boy cares about is even more important than what he knows. How a boy feels toward himself and toward other people can be of more significance than his actual performance at the moment. In working with a boy we need to guide the development and expression of attitudes in relationships with the people around him, for these attitudes and ways of reacting are liable to become lifelong habits.

Mastery of Skills

As a boy learns a new skill, he gains a deepened sense of self-confidence. The Scout learns to pitch his tent, to build his fire, to cook his food—and to enjoy his new-found skills.

He begins to feel more at home in the open, less unsure of himself. He becomes a capable swimmer and learns to paddle a canoe. His fears are transformed into a sense of sureness of himself in his world, a feeling of being ready for whatever may come. He is able to camp in all kinds of weather because he has learned how, because he is prepared. He climbs mountain trails and takes each new difficulty in his stride.

Meeting these tests of his skill and of himself has made him a stronger person. The man in the boy has met the mountain. He keeps climbing more challenging trails.

Finding Himself and His World

Imagine that you are going along a street and you find a man who has lost his way. Suppose you say to him, "You are really not lost, you are at Twelfth and G Streets. I know where you are." You say to yourself "I have found him," and you move on totally oblivious of your superficial analysis.

Obviously your finding him is utterly useless, for he is still lost! You cannot find him! Yet you might have guided him in such a way that he could have found himself. You might have pointed out a landmark which was familiar to him. You might have pointed out the Capitol and St. Albans and the towering Washington Monument. With these direction points you could have guided him so that he could have found himself.

This is largely the procedure of the wise leader of youth. He points out by what he *is* and what he does, often in very incidental ways, some of the landmarks of manliness. Then gradually the boy begins to discover himself and the values of the world in which he lives.

Advancement Values

A strong program of good practical Scouting in patrol, troop, and district *can* lead to advancement. Scout rank needs to be dealt with as important and highly desirable. We must not belittle advancement as a "mere by-product." It is a symbol of something the boy has achieved, a symbol of far-reaching values.

We do not want to confuse the value with the measure of the value. Nor do we want to defeat the acquiring of the value by playing down the attractive symbol by which we recognize the value acquired.

Growing in stature and advancement in spirit, in participation, and in Scoutcraft skills, are the very heart of Scouting procedures. We need to accent them and emphasize them.

A Better Trail to Follow

"Twenty years ago a boy in that particular section of Detroit had one chance in three of landing in the penitentiary," a community leader pointed out. Then he added, "That has been changed since the Detroit Police Department has set up a Scout troop in each precinct of the city.

"They take many boys who have started on the wrong trail, into their police sponsored troops, but in an overwhelming percentage of cases, through their Scouting experiences, these boys discover a better trail to follow."

An Eagle Scout—So What?

"An Eagle Scout—so what?" a chance acquaintance asked, not really meaning to belittle something strong and good.

" 'So what?' you ask," an earnest man replied. "Let me tell you, friend, some of the 'so what.' First a boy must be a Scout —and that takes something pretty fine inside him. He doesn't get to be a Scout by accident. He has to choose that path.

"That simple choosing means that he wants to count, *with* purposes, people, and worthwhile causes, to do his share to advance the common good. No, don't go. You asked, 'So what?' Now hear me out.

"If he is one in twenty, he'll climb to be a First Class Scout. That's no cinch. He'll get there by always keeping going. Oh, you understand something of what a First Class Scout is? Good.

"Of course, it's more than what you do. It's what you are. One out of every ten or so who persevere to First Class rank goes on to Star.

"Oh, you have to go? You can't wait to hear? I'm sorry, for I'd like for you to really understand that an Eagle Scout

69

is truly something special, worth all the pride that we can have and show for him."

I'm grateful for this incident in which my thoughtless friend spoke those words that aroused me so.

"An Eagle Scout—so what!"

Someday I hope to talk to him again. Perhaps he'll tell me then that he, too, feels a touch of pride for this tall-grown boy with purpose in his stride, this Eagle Scout.

Concerned to Understand

Youth need to grow to understand quite a few significant concerns more fully. They need to learn the importance of the dignity of every man. Youth need to realize that the respect they feel for a person usually shows through and becomes part of their influence and relationships. They need to see the importance of peace in the hearts of men, for until it is established there, we will not have peace among community groups or among the nations of the world.

Youth need to realize that there is real satisfaction in work. Work is not something to be avoided or dreaded. It is not punishment or the price we pay. It is our means of high usefulness and deep satisfaction.

Youth need to realize early in life that struggle is normal, that very little is gained without effort and the expenditure of energy.

Recognize the law as a friend. Understand the reason for the law and work in harmony with it. Realize that force and violence are not the means of accomplishing progress. We go forward through evolution, not through revolution.

Find a need and meet it. When you see something that needs to be accomplished in the world, analyze the situation and see whether or not this is a field in which you can help.

We need to balance the sciences and the humanities. During the last twenty years we have made much more progress in the scientific fields than we have in the fields of human engineering. There are many vocations in public service that are opening up and that may appeal.

Wildernesses Still to Conquer

"I don't know what's the matter with you lately, Jim," his father had said the night before. Perhaps the man had meant little by it, perhaps it was merely a gesture of impatience, but the boy had thought deeply about it, and the thought had disturbed his sleep.

"Dad, I think I've figured out what's the matter with me," the boy greeted his father in a most matter-of-fact tone the next morning at breakfast.

"Figured out what's the matter with you—why I didn't know you weren't feeling well, James," his mother exclaimed.

"Oh, I feel all right, but Dad said last night that he couldn't figure out what ailed me lately, and I've thought it over and—and—"

A quizzical look settled on the father's face. Even Jimmie's older brother looked up interestedly.

Then with just a note of mystery in his voice and manner, for boyhood is instinctively, unconsciously dramatic, Jimmie announced, "I think I have a *restless soul!*"

Father and Mother put forth special efforts to look solemn. Jimmie's older brother held his napkin to his mouth to hide a spontaneous smile.

"I've been reading about Daniel Boone and Kit Carson and Sam Houston. The story says that they were men of restless souls. I guess maybe my soul's restless too. The trouble is that I haven't any wildernesses left to conquer."

A startled father cleared his throat. "Jim, I guess you're right about your restless soul. Most boys' souls are restless, I think. But you're mistaken about there not being any wildernesses left to conquer. You're full of wildernesses, and life is full of wildernesses."

"Where, Dad?" Jimmy was eager, but there was a note of suspicion in his voice.

"Don't you worry about wildernesses to conquer. School is something of a wilderness. Down at the plant there are a lot of undiscovered and unconquered problems. Too many men are not happy in their work. Some people are quarreling. All these are the wildernesses of today, Son."

A Scout Advances

We never *make* a Scout pass requirements. In fact, we don't talk to a Scout about the requirements very much.

Lead a horse to water, let him see the water, let him watch other horses drinking, and you don't have to *make* him drink.

Just bring a Scout face-to-face with a chance to learn new lore. Make it a pleasant and happy experience, and you need not worry much about his getting it. Give boys plenty of *uses* for signaling, first aid, and map-making, and they will soon be able to meet any advancement requirements.

Give a boy knowledge of the tools, teach him how to use them, and you'll be surprised at the results!

The New Scout Builds an Equity in His Troop

When a boy becomes a Scout, his enthusiasm at joining is high. The troop's natural momentum and its colorful program of activities are usually compelling enough to assure devoted participation for some time on his part and on the part of his parents.

Then after several months there often comes a crucial period. "His interest begins to lag," we say. His patrol and troop procedures may sometimes seem less colorful to him than they did at first. The Scout may begin to miss an occasional meeting.

What is the remedy?

We need to do everything possible right from his first day as a Scout to make sure that this new boy in the troop begins to *build up his equity in Scouting.*

The man who owns a house is going to be more proud of it and more devoted to improving it than the man who merely rents it. Small equity or large, a man is more inclined to value, take care of, and feel satisfaction in the possession of that house. The Scout in the troop in a similar way can build up his equity in Scouting.

A boy can build several kinds of equities in his Scout troop, one of which is an equity in rank. If he becomes a First Class Scout, he has more to lose by dropping out than if he is only a Tenderfoot. If he has three merit badges, he is more likely to stay than if he has none.

His experience in patrol and troop can help him make friends and feel so strong a sense of fellowship in his Scouting relationships that he just naturally keeps them growing.

There are equities in rank in leadership, in the sense of satisfaction in learning and understanding about Scouting. The deeper his roots go, the higher his interest will reach.

Help each new boy to build far-flung equities in Scouting.

Motivation

How would you arouse a boy's interest in a rowboat? You would probably give him an opportunity to have considerable contact with a boat. You would provide opportunity for him to work with the oars and develop *self-assurance* and *satisfaction* in the use of the boat.

Similarly, we might ask the question, "How would you arouse a boy's interest in trustworthiness?" Probably through contact with this quality in its most definite, most practical form. We would want the boy to have *actual experience* with others who are trustworthy. We would want him to face *actual situations* in which he would naturally respond in a trustworthy way.

Widened Horizons

There has been too much of a tendency in American life for youth to grow up inside the walls of our smug villages and suburbs with relatively little contact with the next town, the next county, or the next state. Through Scouting, however, boys now come together in rallies, Courts of Honor, and in camp, from many types of towns and communities. Their horizons become wider.

Occasionally they come together from considerable distances at National and World Jamborees.

Representative Scouts gather every four years in a world friendships rally or jamboree. These opportunities for widened horizons and for building national and international goodwill can be far-reaching.

Values Through Experiences

From many dozen, perhaps from hundreds of experiences, a boy decides that he would like to be a particular kind of man. He is a pretty demanding taskmaster, even for himself. He is outspoken in his dislikes. He admires deeply but impatiently scoffs at imitations and at what seems superficial to him.

What is the significance of this value-building process to Scouters? It means that we must try at every turn to surround each boy with as many reinforcing experiences as possible, those situations involving the making of choices, deciding, analyzing, evaluating, and using judgment.

Chapter 5

Developing Skill
with People

**A BOY HAS MANY PROBLEMS, MANY NEEDS,
AND NUMEROUS POINTS OF CONFUSION. MANY
OF THESE BAFFLING RELATIONSHIPS CENTER
AROUND HIS UNDERSTANDING OF PEOPLE. HIS
HAPPINESS AND HIS SUCCESS IN THE WORLD WILL
DEPEND IN NO SMALL MEASURE ON HOW SKILL-
FULL HE BECOMES IN DEALING WITH PEOPLE.**

No single facet of the Scout leader's overall opportunity
stands out more clearly than the super-special need to help
boys develop concern for people and unusual skill in dealing
with them.

The Scout leader needs to develop his own skill in dealing
with people and to keep it growing. As he demonstrates it in
living with boys, somehow they will develop similar ways of
treating people. This is a skill that rubs off on people.

The basic attitude is to feel a genuine concern for people.
On this we build the human relations aptitudes that make the
difference in our relationships with them. A team is made
up of basic attitudes of goodwill and skilled aptitudes of
good living.

How Does He Get Along with People?

And there is this question—does this Scout get along with people? He has phoned Mr. Barnes for a merit badge appointment, and Mr. Barnes is out of town. He has phoned Mr. Jones and found that his phone is disconnected. Impatiently he has said, "I quit. Too much red tape. I didn't want to qualify for a photography merit badge anyway."

The procedures of making appointments, of keeping them on time, of meeting new people, are vital experiences possible for a Scout. Let's hope that boys may have some little inconveniences occasionally in finding a merit badge counselor. Let's hope that occasionally the counselor will say, "John, you've made a good start, but you're not ready for my O.K. on this yet. Better come back for a further session."

These situations are real. They are life. If John sulks and quits in the face of them, he is likely to be headed for a lifetime of sulking and quitting.

In such situations wise parents and understanding Scout leaders will help John to see life as an adventure, not always easy, not always simple, but still an adventure calling for enthusiasm and perseverance.

How does John get along with people? He is out of patience with his patrol leader and says he is going to quit. All his life he will have superiors with whom he could lose patience and so feel tempted to quit. But the world is impatient with quitters.

There is probably no point of possible grief at which understanding parents and leaders can help John more than at the critical point of adjusting himself to the difficultness of other human beings with whom he must deal.

As time goes on he will learn, if he is observant and thoughtful, how to manage people, how to get them to work with him. When he has learned how to get along with people, he will find that he has gained new powers of leadership and management which result in persons' being more ready to help him.

A Scoutmaster with Patience

Suppose you have been carrying on a drive for neater uniforming in your troop. You have a conviction that if a boy is neat and looks like a Scout on the outside, he will be more likely to catch the feeling of being a real Scout on the inside. Suppose every boy in your troop owns a uniform and you are making a concerted effort to make sure that every boy wears his uniform to the meeting. Suppose you are Scoutmaster Pete Scott, Troop 117, of Peter E. Howell School Parent-Teachers Association, Tucson, Arizona.

Ten minutes after the meeting starts, in comes Bill, purposely dressed for the occasion. He is wearing bedroom slippers, a Hawaiian shirt, torn jeans, a huge Mexican hat. His posture is such that his head is twelve inches farther forward than his toes.

Of course the troop roars! The scene is truly funny, but everybody understands that this is a deliberate attempt to get a laugh at the troop's expense.

The Scoutmaster asks himself, "Is this an attempt to make a laughing stock of me and of the troop? What can we do that would be most helpful in straightening out this young man?"

Then he speaks directly to the boy: "Go home. Stay home. You're a disgrace to Scouting. With your present attitude, I can't see that our efforts will be rewarded. Time is pretty scarce and too valuable to spend on a guy with your attitude," he says. The colorfully draped boy stalks deliberately toward the door.

The following night the boy comes to the Scoutmaster's home with an apology. The Scoutmaster accepts him coolly and invites him to the next meeting if he really feels that he can conduct himself like a Scout.

Willing to do whatever he can to help the boy, but still not fully convinced, Scoutmaster Scott contacts various men who know Bill to try to learn of some interest or some handle which he may take hold of in order to get next to the real boy. In searching, the Scoutmaster learns that Bill is proficient in using the Morse code. Signaling also just happens to be one of the troop's weak points.

As time passes, the Scoutmaster puts the boy in charge of signaling instruction in the troop where he does an excellent job. The boy has taken on a new lease of life in the troop. He no longer has to get attention by showing off and by causing trouble. He no longer feels the need to put on a show. He has found a genuine way of getting recognition.

A year later the boy moves away, but the Scoutmaster still receives letters from him. Occasionally there comes a word of appreciation and thanks, a significant paycheck in a Scoutmaster's life.

When the boy comes back to Tucson for an occasional visit, he seldom fails to contact his old Scoutmaster.

"I merely searched for a handle to take hold of, for an interest on which I could build. When you once find that contact point, helping the boy becomes easy," Scoutmaster Scott explains.

Getting Parents to Help

Scout leaders sometimes get discouraged for many reasons, momentarily, but my guess is that no one thing makes them feel more down-to-earth month after month than the failure of parents to take part in the activities in the troop to which they are invited.

Too often when a parents' night is poorly attended, the Scoutmaster feels like throwing up his hands and asking himself, "Oh! What's the use?" But a Scout leader—and the troop —have too much at stake for him to quit trying!

He keeps on trying again and again; he learns more about promotion methods and about getting boys to help "sell" Scouting to their own parents and about involving adults in helping. Then before long the time comes when he begins to see the parents of his Scouts getting behind the troop and pushing! Then it is only one step further until they are out in front of the troop *pulling!*

We Went Fishing Together

(As told to Walter MacPeek by a Scoutmaster.)

"I wish I could find an assistant Scoutmaster like yours, Bob. You certainly have a good teamwork relationship with him. You're lucky," a fellow Scouter said to me not long ago.

I smiled because only a year before, Dick and I hadn't been hitting things off especially well.

We had no outright breaks, yet I couldn't help but sense a kind of holding back on Dick's part. His response to my requests had seemed a bit grudging, more in manner and attitude than in anything you could put your finger on.

I felt the tension growing between us, and I knew that we couldn't make progress that way. Before long an incident would develop, and then—

Recognizing that we were almost to the breaking point, I had an inspiration one day. "Dick," I said, "How would you like to go fishing with me?"

Dick was surprised. "Why—yes—I'd like to go," he said.

As we drove out to the fishing spot, Dick told me a bit about his family and his job. He was having a financial struggle at home. He had been working under a good deal of tension at the factory and was glad to open up and talk about some of his troubles. I listened and showed my genuine interest and concern.

I had not fully realized how much of an extra burden Dick's work with the troop had sometimes been to him. Once, he told me, he had been detained at the factory and had come to our meeting without his supper—he had just eaten a sandwich on the run.

As I listened I felt increasingly guilty, for I had a feeling that I had not shown very much appreciation to Dick for his help. I had taken it pretty much for granted as a service due me because I work hard as a Scoutmaster too.

Then I opened up to Dick, admitted that I had not shown much appreciation, and he asked, "Well, am I really much help to you? Is what I do really of much importance?"

Well, you can see how Dick and I really began to get acquainted—down underneath—that day. From that day on we have been a team.

I don't remember whether or not we caught many fish on that trip, but I do know that I discovered a solid-gold assistant Scoutmaster—and a new friend.

Yep—I'm lucky!

They Will Remember People

Ask a man who was a Scout years ago about the experiences and events he recalls and pretty soon he will tell you about his old Scoutmaster or some other man in Scouting who influenced him, perhaps a merit badge counselor or a leader in camp.

Rudolph M. Wittenberg says in *So You Want to Help People:*

"The boys behave better in Tom's tinker-shop partly because nobody else ever showed them how to fix a radio, partly because they like and respect Tom. There is something intangible between a leader and a group that goes much deeper than the knowledge and skill he brings. Years after youngsters have forgotten where they learned to fix a radio, or to make a belt, or to play in an orchestra, or to preside in a meeting, they will remember Tom—and that will *make a difference in how they think and feel and act.*"

Guidance

A boy with tingling memories of his failure to do what he was told to do walked down the street. "I just won't get caught next time," the boy told himself, while back in the house the father, totally uncomprehending his ineffective methods of control, mumbled, "Hope he learned his lesson."

But the only lesson the boy had learned was a wrong one. The father had made no gain in the boy's understanding, and he had lost ground in his relationship with his son.

Getting the Feel of the Wheel

"When my boy was sixteen," my friend said to me, "I started teaching him to drive. For many months we drove together. Then when he was eighteen, after we had driven together for many hundreds of miles, he began driving by himself."

In less than fifty words this big man had told me a story of untold hours of work—of going along on a lot of trips which he probably did not particularly enjoy.

But he wanted his boy to "get the feel of the wheel" and thus be prepared for a lifetime of safe driving. Such a father-

and-son program of learning to drive would drastically cut America's accident toll.

And a father-and-son program of facing problems and weighing values, of getting the "feel of the wheel" of life, would cut America's heartbreak toll even more. Wanted: more fathers to try it.

Chapter 6

Searching for Values

WHEN A BOY OR YOUNG MAN BEGINS TO DE-
VELOP A SENSE OF MATURITY, HE HAS GONE A
LONG WAY. THAT FRIEND AND COUNSELOR WHO
HELPS A BOY TO SEARCH FOR VALUES, TO EVALU-
ATE POSSIBLE CHOICES, POINTS HIM TOWARD A
BEGINNING SENSE OF MATURITY.

Growing up is not an easy nor a simple process. Attaining maturity is a many-sided process depending upon numerous factors, some of which can be quite elusive.

A boy does not grow up overnight, nor does he always attain a point on the trail toward maturity that he is sure to hold. Sometimes he slips back. Sometimes he regresses. But even more often he may astound his mentors by the progress he makes.

The great desire in his heart is to be treated as a person of worth and respected for his maturity, for being an individual. But the process of growing up stretches over many years. He is a fortunate boy who counts among his friends several Scout leaders who let him know that they respect him and believe in him and who encourage him to search for basic life values.

Doing His Best

As he takes part in his Scouting activities, a boy forms the habit of doing his best. Experiences in patrol and troop open the door to greater happiness and satisfaction for him. He finds that the ideal of doing his best in everything he tackles will lead to helpful and satisfying friendships.

"It's going to be right—my very best," he says as he works at the task time and again.

"Know-how plus caring enough" is his formula.

Specifications

How does a boy go about choosing and building ideas of the measurements and specifications for the kind of man he would like to be? Does he sometimes fashion them as he sits around the campfire? Or perhaps as he follows the trail up a mountainside? Or in the give-and-take of working and planning with his patrol? Or perhaps as he sits quietly reading a book or magazine?

Influence

An unassuming blind man, Jesse Bailey, a dishwasher at the Louisiana State School for the Blind, died several years ago. He had grown up an orphan in the school for the blind, never having known his parents. In 1923 be became a charter member of the new Scout troop formed at the school. When Jesse finished his schooling, he stayed on as a kitchen helper and dishwasher and became a friend to every boy in the school.

During his life Jesse Bailey developed three enthusiasms: one for his church, one for Scouting, and the other for helping the youngsters in the school. He spent several summers in Scout camp, and with his guitar and his harmonica he became a favorite among the boys of the camp.

When he died some years ago, the proceeds of a small insurance policy paid for his burial expenses and left in addition a little more than $1,000 to be used to provide Christmas parties for the children of the school. Most of the youngsters of the school go home at Christmastime, but a few of them who have no home to go to or who live far from the school stay on.

When the Lions Club of Baton Rouge heard of the legacy of happiness that Jesse Bailey had left to his blind friends, they decided to keep the fund intact and use only the income from it. They took over the management of the annual Christmas party, and each year they make up whatever balance is needed. Jesse Bailey showed them the way.

And so the influence of this humble, greathearted man lives on.

We Live as Long

We will continue to be very much alive as long as those influences which we have helped to set up shall continue to enrich and brighten human life. When our foresight is so alert and full of understanding that we gladly bequeath a part of our substance "to serve our purpose long after we are gone," the generation coming after us is indeed a fortunate one, and we live on forever.

Legacy

So many men of days gone by have left rich legacies of uplifting thought, ennobling purpose, and tangible substance so greatly beneficial to me, that I count it no generosity on my part that I, in turn, strive to help create a legacy for future generations. Thus I pass on to those who follow some small part of what I have gained from others. It is only fair, merely a part of the debt which I owe to the oncoming tomorrow.

Merit Badge Counselors

More than a million and a half times last year a merit badge counselor sat down with a boy, reviewed an area of knowledge with him, and finally wrote his signature to certify that this particular boy had met the requirements of the merit badge they had considered together.

Who are these merit badge counselors? They are an enthusiastic group of devoted men with widely varying interests and backgrounds. Some of them are dyed-in-the-wool Scouters, and others are relatively unfamiliar with Scouting procedures. Yet they have knowledge and background in a special field, and they are happy to share this understanding with boys who are eager to learn something of that field.

Take a veteran Scouter in Massachusetts, for instance. He is a retired executive of a utilities company, a man who is alive and alert to everything around him.

He can tell you the general plan of the drainage of the water from the rolling hills of his area. Boys open their eyes wide as he makes the most commonplace-looking item take on special interest and fascination for them.

"You never go to see him but that you learn something you never thought of before," an Eagle Scout explained, "and if you don't know what you need to know, he helps you find out about it. He has a lot of patience. You sort of feel that he enjoys having you come. He's never in a hurry or too busy."

When a boy comes for an interview on a safety merit badge, another merit badge counselor gets down an old flintlock gun, and they look it over together. The wide-eyed Scout is thinking of the gun. The man beside him is thinking about using this firearm to help get across the principles of gun safety to the boy beside him. He uses his unusual collection of varieties of woods in a similar way. He understands that boys learn from concrete articles which they can see and handle.

Another counselor has a collection of *Boys' Life* and *Scouting* magazines which go back for more than forty years, and he is generous in lending copies to Scouts and to Scouters who want to dig into a particular subject.

"Sure I keep a record of who I lend them to. If they don't return them in a reasonable time, I let them know. It's a part of their training. And besides I need the magazine for the next fellow," he explains.

Does it take time to be a merit badge counselor? "Surely it does, but what better use can a man make of his time?" the former mayor of Seattle commented when I asked him about his evenings spent in counseling boys in various merit badges. "It's a happy experience to have these wide-awake youngsters phone for an interview, then show up for our visit together," a veteran merit badge counselor in Grand Rapids, Michigan, and dean of merit badge counselors there observed, "It's not just a matter of finding out if a boy is qualified for a merit badge. It's also an opportunity to make a new friend —maybe sometimes to give a boy a little bit of added encouragement."

Encouraging the Growth of Ideals

The ideals of Scouting have to do with life, with the level upon which its men and boys live and the yet higher levels toward which they strive. These Scouting ideals point upward to high quality in physical fitness; in responsible, participating citizenship; and in the growth of integrity of personal qualities.

Self-action (not waiting to be towed) is the force we need to get started in many boys through example, counsel, encouragement, and challenge, while they are having fun in Scouting activities.

By *encouraging* desirable action and through the use of *group approval* and group tradition we often influence the standards by which a boy lives.

Practicing the Good Turn tends to develop habits of caring enough about others to help them. Working together with boys of many creeds and races in the democratic patrol and troop group helps to develop genuine social consciousness in boys. Community service with its attendant satisfaction can be as effective in practice as it is in theory.

Scouting has developed an enviable record for the development of valuable skills, based on careful know-how training for leaders and boys. The keynote has been to help boys to learn to "Be Prepared" through actual opportunities made as lifelike as possible.

We need to concern ourselves with human relations, with the ways we treat people. Disappointing interpersonal relationships in Scouting cause many to "lose interest." If we can make the things the boy ought to do satisfying to him and those he ought not to do annoying, we have solved many of the problems of his growing up.

We adults need to do a careful job in living the ideals we preach in order that boys may catch the full values possible.

Contagion of Character in Camp

A boy's character is most often influenced by the subtle impact of a personality in action. The boy's standards of judgment, of conduct, of idealism, are often pretty definitely focused and crystallized by the unspoken, sometimes unconscious influence of a man or another boy.

The power to brighten or darken human life, the influence of a leader who lives on a high level of idealism instead of on a sodden plane of mere existence, is so far-reaching that we who are responsible for selecting leaders of boys' groups must often search our own souls to ask ourselves whether or not we have searched hard enough for those men of finest grain, of strongest character, to be the leaders of our boys.

Perhaps there have been times when we have been too much occupied with menus and equipment and program and nature study, all of which are of considerable importance, —and not enough concerned in the selection of the personnel of our man power. "Just any man" will not do.

A period at camp is often the most intimate, most far-reaching influence in the life of a boy. Under unskilled, unconsecrated, or unconscious leadership, there are probably very few character values inherent in camp life.

The caliber of manliness of the leader, his vision, his high purpose, his human sympathetic understanding of boy nature —ever beset with turbulent confusions and problems—are essential to the man who is to lead boys.

Through camping experiences boys of promise live in contact with men of high character. But with second-rate, mediocre men in contact with boys of promise, the result is that of influencing boys to become only second-rate, mediocre men. We must not be satisfied with men who may fall short. Boys grow to be like the men with whom they live. Perhaps our foremost opportunities to influence boy character come through ensuring campers of frequent contact with men of high character, men of greatest spiritual outlook and outreach.

Mere Building of Personal Popularity

That leader who has as his aim merely securing the affection of his boys does not have an adequate picture of his task. The effective Scoutmaster must of course have the respect of his boys. If he concerns himself with the needs of boys and the providing of Scouting experiences for his patrols, meeting these needs in a fair and friendly manner, he need give no extra thought to securing the friendliness of his boys. Popularity alone is no great achievement, and it is an aim unworthy of a great leader. The enrichment of the lives of boys—seeing their needs and serving them—is the great challenging opportunity of the Scout leader.

Scouting education is built on the basic principle that boys teach themselves and each other. The Scoutmaster is primarily a manager rather than a teacher. The most effective teacher in a troop is often a towheaded youngster with an army of freckles camping on his nose.

The leader of a group of boys may merely point the trail ahead, possibly pointing to the dim outline of a mountain objective in the far distance. He can even travel along the trail with the group, but he can never travel the trail for them. Each boy must climb his own mountain! Growth into higher understanding is a task which no one can do for him.

Legacy for a Son

Son, in the years ahead it will be only natural that you will recall some of our times together. You'll think back to your dad, much as I sometimes think back to mine.

We've been pretty good friends. Oh, sometimes I may have seemed a bit stern, but all in all I've tried to be a pretty understanding and approachable father. I hope I haven't failed you.

Remember our camping trips, Son? I pretended to get a kick out of them, but I had a feeling even then that I wasn't fooling you. My frame somehow didn't adjust too well to the ground, but still I think those trips were worthwhile because of the chance you and I had to spend some time with each other as two good friends.

Now I hope that your inheritance will be adequate to meet the needs of the days ahead. I never accumulated as much money as I might have—perhaps not as much as I should have. Somehow property and money never seemed of highest importance.

So, instead of money, I leave to you the freedom to choose your own work and the thrill of building your own fortune.

It's likely that someday you will have a son. You and his mother will give up a lot of pleasures and plans to meet the demands of that boy. You'll be puzzled sometimes—not just sure what kind of heritage you will leave him.

So, Son, I leave the whole world to you. Face it as an adventure. Live each day at your best, one day at a time.

Leadership Traits to Encourage

A leader is one who influences others. When he speaks, people listen. When he goes somewhere, others just want to go along with him. But why? What are the traits that make for this influence in an individual?

How can we spot and encourage promising leadership qualities in others? Are there some learnable leadership skills that we should strive to analyze? You have often asked yourself many of these questions. This area of leadership growth is important to you in your personal growth and in your management of others.

Watch for the person who just naturally takes charge of an emergency situation which comes up unexpectedly. What is the basis of this taking charge?—Previous experience, a sense of caring for the good of the group, or the fact that others seem naturally to look to him to take over.

Observe people discussing a problem. When Joe advances an idea, the others almost invariably listen. When Bill makes a suggestion, it is often given scant heed. This is a leadership situation, effective or ineffective, depending upon various factors. What are they?

Sometimes the person selected to do a job is not the person with most influence with the group. Sometimes he does not know what he is trying to do or how to accomplish his aims. How important are the recognition of goals as a part of a man's leadership influence?

What are the implications in this of the management of our community groups? Leadership skill, unfortunately, is not always linked with constructive helpfulness. Leadership ability can sometimes be used for wrong ends. What can we do about this? Must we link up some other qualities with leadership performance?

Here is a list of some abilities to look for in trying to spot men who promise leadership ability of a high order:

Is he liked and respected?

Does he influence others?

Can he take charge of the group?

Can he handle individuals?

Can he iron out difficulties?

Do others look to him when decisions need to be made?

Is he enthusiastic, responsible, constructive?

Guardrails

When I interviewed Fred B. Dickson, then warden of San Quentin Penitentiary, he said, "Home filled with conflict and low standards, ruthless attitudes toward life values, argument, discord, and misunderstanding—that's a picture of the boyhood background of a great many of the men here at San Quentin.

"A boy needs to have a feeling of security, of stability, of belonging. It is hard for him to get this deep-down feeling of his own significance to the world in a home life of rejection, or overdominant or overpermissive family life. An adolescent needs to have guard rails to bump up against, to warn him, to help him cut down on his quota of mistakes, and to help straighten him out when he makes a mistake."

In Days Ahead

"That boy—what can you see in him? He interrupts, gets so out of hand, and doesn't seem to show respect for what you do for him," a friend commented, referring to this loud-lunged boy, adding, "He's noisy, and he won't sit still. His hair is mussed, and his clothes are all awry."

I paused for quite a while before I spoke, "I guess your're right—at least about the outside of the boy. I'd never really noticed—at least not much—his interruptions and his lack of bowing down to honor my gray hairs. But I *have* noticed that he's in earnest all the way.

"And through his loudness and the havoc that he makes, sometimes I see a man striding forward, a man who'll greatly need strong ruggedness to face the days ahead. Mussed-up hair and clothes awry? I'm sure that they can be brushed and straightened up. And have you seen how he holds on— refusing to be pushed aside—how time after time he makes a point and drives it home till all agree?

"When I look at Tom, I don't look back at past mistakes. I try to look ahead to days to come—to days that need the strength of men who'll carry loads and swing the hammer hard and straight. I see in this young giant looming tall, the hope and promise of days ahead as he stands rugged and faces forward."

As Boys Grow

Men have come into Scouting because of many and varied enthusiasms, but those who have stayed any significant length of time have usually been those who have developed a desire to *encourage the growth of boys* into citizens of high character.

A man who is primarily enthusiastic about handicraft or athletics or any other skill *for its own sake* does not usually continue long in Scouting. However, the man who is primarily interested in the physical, mental, and moral growth of the boy, in encouraging his all-round development—finds the Scouting programs a helpful tool to aid in the accomplishment of these objectives.

In addition to the significant contribution that Scouting experiences make to the individual boy, there are many people who rate high the effects of Scouting on the growth of adults and the growth of family life and the development of community and national pride, teamwork, and morale.

What Is He Being Led Into?

"We've kept our boy out of trouble fairly well. He doesn't smoke or chew or drink or do other things that harm. As a youngster we kept him off the streets and out of scrapes and soon he'll be a *Man*."

"All that is good," I said, "but not enough. You've told me what he doesn't do. That's fine as far as it can go. But I want to know what he *does* do. I'm glad he isn't into trouble, but what *is* he in to? From what you say he isn't harmful or destructive. But next to that, the worst I know is being neutral.

"Is he a man who *helps* his town? Does he aid in good enterprises as they come along? Does he reflect and consider matters thoughtfully? Does he treat his fellowmen with fairness and give each man his due?

Is he growing in his life and work? When his end comes, will America be a better place because he lived?

"I'm glad he's not against America. But I hope he's not neutral to the life about him either. No, it's not enough to keep him 'out of' things or 'off the streets.' We've got to lead him *into* values, too."

Too Much Egress!

It is recorded that P. T. Barnum, in order to keep people moving out of his sideshows to make room for others to come in, once had huge signs beckoning people "This way to the Egress." Many people wondered just what sort of animal the Egress was, followed the sign, and were startled to find themselves outside.

We have altogether too much "egress" in Scouting—a good deal of it, too, in an even less dignified way than the Barnum method! Too many boys go out of Scouting into *nothing*. They merely egress! Too many boys do not definitely leave the troop. They just "ooze" out. Often with a bit of a shock a boy realizes that he is no longer a member of his old troop! He has been dropped without having had a real chance to decide whether or not he wanted to be dropped.

Of course, we should help every Scout realize that "once a Scout" he is "always a Scout," although he may no longer be on the membership rolls of his old Troop.

Sentimental ties can be strong. Some Scouts, when they go away to school, continue their registrations with the old troop and still "carry on" where they can.

Certainly we do not want a boy merely to "egress" out

of the troop, even when he must become inactive. We want his ceremony of leaving to be a happy, eventful going. As a part of that ceremony we want to impress him that he is only *temporarily* leaving active service in his troop and that in his heart he will continue to be as much a Scout as he ever was—and that someday he will be coming back as a Scouter!

Chapter 7

Discovering
Inner Resources

A SCOUT LEADER SHOWS RESPECT FOR WHAT
A BOY IS, FOR WHAT HE IS BECOMING, AND FOR
WHAT HE *MIGHT* BECOME.

A Scout leader always treats a boy as a person of worth, potential and not yet demonstrated. He helps a boy discover his own strengths and possibilities—especially his inner resources. He encourages a boy to build on these strengths.

How can you encourage a person to develop his inner resources? How can a Scout leader help a boy realize the potential of these inner strengths that he can draw upon? He can do this by living with him, by sharing with him, and by showing trust, confidence, and expectancy of good.

Toward Conscious Unity of Self

In every boy's daily conduct there are incidents of contradictory behavior. As he matures, his life becomes more unified, and the contradictions become less frequent.

The boy often needs help during the period of gradually unfolding consciousness through which he is going. Our task consists of helping him become more conscious of the many powers at work around him and especially more conscious of himself and his own power.

Leaders of youth can reinforce boys' lives so that those who come under their leadership will not fail to adapt and adjust to situations. We can help boys develop conscious *unity of self*.

A Boy Needs to Believe in Himself

In all the world there seemed to be no place for Bill. His father had deserted the family, and after an exhausting day at the factory, Bill's mother was often impatient and irritable.

"Aw, what's the use? I just don't matter," Bill told himself over and over.

One night, halfheartedly and almost expecting to be rebuffed, he went to a Scout troop meeting in his neighborhood. The Scoutmaster gave him a friendly welcome, assigned him to a patrol, and introduced him to other boys.

As the weeks went by, Bill showed special skill in handicraft. Soon he was instructing other Scouts in how to make things with their hands. He had patience and teaching skill as well as the ability to see possibilities in a scrap of wood. He began to feel wanted and needed.

Bill, a grown-up now, is not a teacher, nor does he count himself as more than an average citizen, but he does credit finding a place for himself in a Scout troop as the first step in finding a useful place for himself in his world.

Experiences That Stir the Hearts of Boys

Do you sometimes wonder what they see, these tall, bronzed boys of ours at camporee? Sometimes, I'm told, they see the Indian braves whose moccasined feet trod upon that same leaf-carpeted forest floor long years ago. Some nights they see the Scouts of other lands, with kilts and turbans and hiking sticks. Sometimes on magic carpet spread they travel back to the days of Washington at Valley Forge, to trails trod by Coronado, and to the site of the Alamo.

These summer evenings coming on will mean more camp-fires with more eager boys with man-sized dreams and king-sized hopes gathered 'round to ponder things they see as flames leap high.

Our Horizons Grew Wider

I am glad my Scoutmaster did not preach to us. I am afraid he would have lessened his influence if he had. He used other more resultful methods.

Now don't think that he was not thoughtful in his approach to his job. He was direct and dramatic, and he pounded away at helping us realize many real values. But he made us reach for them.

I remember one night at a campfire when he quoted these four lines from James Russell Lowell:

> When I was a beggarly boy,
> And lived in a cellar damp,
> I had not a friend nor a toy,
> But I had Aladdin's lamp;
> When I could not sleep for the cold,
> I had fire enough in my brain,
> And builded, with roofs of gold,
> My beautiful castles in Spain!

The setting was just right. We did not think poetry out of place there. We did not ask him what the point was. He did not insult us by explaining. But somehow he got something across to us.

I remember another time when a half dozen of us were in

camp. We got to talking about how we would like to have a big house or a big car or a lot of money someday.

"That might be OK, but do you know what John Burroughs said?" he asked us. Then he quoted: "'For my part as I grow older, I am more and more inclined to reduce my baggage, to lop off superfluities. I become more and more in love with the simple things and simple folk—a small house, a hut in the woods, a tent on the shore.'"

We did not argue with this point of view. A day or two later I borrowed a book of the writings of John Burroughs and threatened to become a nature philosopher.

Somehow we were flattered that our Scoutmaster considered us grown-up enough to share some of his adult thoughts and various viewpoints with us. I don't believe he ever gave us much direct advice on life values, but he certainly influenced us. We thought it "big stuff" to know some of the good things that important men had said.

Many times a teacher would be informed, "Oh, our Scoutmaster knows all about Kipling,"—or Stevenson or some other writer. Campfires were his great joy. Storytelling was one of his most effective tools. He also loaned us books from his well-stocked library.

Whenever I run across a line of verse from Gerald Gould, even now I can see my old Scoutmaster beside a Michigan lake quoting:

Yonder the long horizon lies, and there by night and day
The old ships draw to home again, the young ships sail away;
And come I may, but go I must, and if men ask you why,
You may put the blame on the stars and the sun and the white
    road and the sky.

I am glad that no two Scoutmasters are alike, but I count myself fortunate to have followed the trail with one who helped introduce us to snatches of mind-stretching wonder and bits of verse that stirred us to want to know and feel more.

Getting Conscious

"Get conscious," the boys on the baseball field yelled at one of their teammates who seemed half asleep.

They did not realize it, but in that direct demand they had summed up a large part of the characteristics of their period of growing up.

Every boy goes through a period of gradual unfoldment. He slowly becomes conscious of the world around and within. Of course he cannot "get conscious" just by being commanded to do so, but gradually he does attain his consciousness. Through friendliness and thoughtful association and by reflection and dreaming and growing up in a happy, helpful setting, sooner or later he will "get conscious."

A boy needs help, patience, counseling, and sometimes a lot of forgiveness in the tempestuous days as he "gets conscious."

She Was a Real Person

I do not recall a single fact that she taught us. Yet, Sunday after Sunday she must have taught us many. I do not remember her as especially learned, yet she may have been. Viewed through the eyes of an adult, she may have been plain and ordinary. But she certainly was not plain and ordinary to a pack of squirming boys! I would not take a big stack of money for what that church-school teacher did for me. Somehow we just knew—felt way down inside—what she wanted from us.

Once or twice a year she would invite us to her home and

fill us up with food, just as she filled our hearts with hope and purpose on Sunday mornings. She did not prove by logic nor convince by argument. She didn't have to. But she built up our inner resources. We just caught something of her goodness and fineness from her. She was a *real person.*

Process and Purpose

It all goes back to purposes. It begins with your purpose and leads to the boy's purpose.

Just what values do we want the boy to develop through his Scouting experiences? Are we primarily interested in getting certain tasks done, or are we chiefly interested in the values *along the way*—the en route values that can come to the boy?

If you were securing a group of temporary workers to straighten a pile of bricks, you might naturally proceed somewhat as a benevolent despot. Of course, you are going to treat your men humanely; you are going to organize the job for efficient procedure. But you are chiefly interested in getting the bricks piled up—in getting the job done.

Now picture another kind of situation. You are still going to pile up bricks, but your chief purpose is something else. Suppose you have selected a half dozen promising young men in your shop—fellows you are grooming to be leaders in your business someday. You are interested in sizing them up—in finding how they get along with others, how they plan and organize a job to be done. In this case you are not primarily concerned with getting the bricks piled up. The chore is only incidental. You are using the task as a process to help you discover human values. You are interested foremost in putting these young men into situations where you can observe them as they plan, organize, and carry through a job. Naturally you would not be a benevolent despot in this situation. You would set up democratic procedures because through them you will bring out the values and the latent capacities in the young men you are developing and measuring.

Scouting is like that—a series of processes which call into play the boys' capacities. The processes give leaders a chance to influence and to encourage the growth of certain abilities and skills. The main objective is not to get a task done but to build a series of good habits through tackling and handling a job.

One Searched for Arrowheads

A leader and a Scout tramped through the woods. They wandered among the high bluffs and cliffs looking for arrowheads. The boy searched earnestly for arrowheads, chatting with the man at his side as they hiked along.

The man, hunting for something far more important than arrowheads, was searching for a vantage point. He was trying to find an interest somewhere deep down inside the boy's heart. He had said to himself, "This boy who is supposed to be difficult to handle can be managed when we get to know him. We must begin with his interests."

What the boy thought was important. How much the boy understood and believed was helpful. Finally the man found the opening he wanted. He discovered the direction of the boy's interest. He discovered the things the boy liked and wanted to know more about.

Together they found a common ground—a mutual affection. The change that came about in the boy's life seemed unbelievable to those who observed, for the observers thought the Scoutmaster merely searched for arrowheads that day he hiked with a boy among the bluffs and cliffs.

They Need to Feel Necessary

"Don't go away feeling you'll be missed" is a taunt sometimes hurled more or less jokingly at an acquaintance as he prepares to leave. An even more devastating challenge would be, "Don't stay around thinking you're necessary."

Back of every failure, regardless of the person's age, is the suspicion—sometimes to the point of obsession—that his efforts are useless, that his work is ineffectual, unappreciated, and unnecessary.

Whenever we help convince a person that he is helpful and worthwhile, we render a significant service. But when we help to convince him that he is "no good," that he is a failure, then we have rendered him a great disservice.

There is no greater factor which contributes to our reaching out to people than the compelling desire to feel necessary.

Lincoln

What a Scoutmaster Lincoln would have made! Picture him in frontier Illinois swinging an ax, instructing a troop of wide-eyed Scouts, leading a singing group on a hike through the woods, or sprawled on a log before the campfire spinning yarns and discussing man's inner longings and yearnings.

Dead for more than a century, Lincoln is more alive today in the hearts and lives of millions of boys than most men who still walk our streets.

What would Lincoln say to us today? What questions would he ask as he sat with his long legs stretched out toward the warming embers of the campfire?

Understanding and Living the Code

Helping boys understand and attain personal goals and ideals is one of the most important phases in the work of a

Scout leader. The Cub Scout learns his motto, his Cub Scout Promise, and the Law of the Cub Pack. Many of his activities in his den and pack are built around learning more about these goals as he finds ways of putting them to use in daily life.

In his patrol and troop the Boy Scout learns and practices living the Scout Oath and Law from day to day. Putting the Good Turn into daily use, quietly and without boasting, is a basic part of the experience of every Scout. In time this procedure becomes an automatic habit, and the Scout just naturally practices the habit of helpfulness.

The ideals of Cub Scouting and Boy Scouting grow naturally into the life values covered in the Explorer Code. This guide for young men helps a youth as more and more he faces directly the responsibilities of adult life.

Influence of a Boy

"I guess what I do is my own affair—why should I worry?" A rebellious youth said in that hotheaded, uncontrolled way not uncommon in the life of a boy not quite fifteen.

"But Bob, what about your influence on others?" The quiet man appeared more patient and unruffled than he really felt underneath as he looked his son squarely in the eye.

"That's a good joke, Dad! My influence on others—I don't have any influence," the boy shot back, a trifle less heatedly than before.

"Son, you can't walk down the street without your shadow falling. That shadow helps or hurts. Your sunshine, you know, Bob?"

"My sunshine? What do you mean, Dad?" Most of the rebellion was gone from his voice now.

"The sun sheds rays that warm and brighten human lives.

Fellows like you are capable of shedding sunshine too, which brightens and warms life."

"Well—maybe, Dad, but who is affected by what I do?"

"The Johnson boy across the street watches you every day, keeps his eye on you as you stride down the street. Remember how you used to look up to and imitate Henry and George?" The father knew that the boy remembered.

The conversation was ended. Father had scored another vic· tory through kind understanding and patience as he helped his son to think things through.

The Difficult to Reach

I often think of what Fred R. Dickson, then warden of San Quentin Penitentiary, told me some years ago. He said, "If I were a Scoutmaster, I'd try to reach more boys from the wrong side of the tracks. I know it's not easy. Their parents sometimes don't help as much as they could. I'd work hard to get close to the boys from tougher neighborhoods. When we once get them on our side, they're a real power. They often eat up Scouting. They put everything they have into it. There is so little in their life that they just naturally put their heart into Scouting activity. Scouting becomes their whole life. They find recognition and achievement. They come to feel they belong. Through Scouting we can often help youngsters rise above the rubble of the life they are raised in."

Growing Up

Scouting in the troop is a *growing-up* program. The Scout is a member, a participant of a patrol. He operates as a member in a democracy. He helps to choose his patrol leader who represents him on the patrol leaders' council. He has a place. He is needed.

107

Lifetime habits are being formed. Ideals are growing. The Scout's sense of loyalty and of personal responsibility is developing. His leaders are striving to provide reinforcing influences and experiences for him. A high code of honor comes alive in his consciousness. Leaders are trying to provide him with numerous opportunities to practice unselfish service and fellowship with other boys and men of strong character.

Important things are happening inside the boy. His Scouting days are truly significant for him.

Chapter 8

Building upon Discipline Values

SCOUTING EXPERIENCES EMPHASIZE THE GROWTH OF THE INDIVIDUAL BOY RATHER THAN THE LEARNING OF ANY PARTICULAR SUBJECT MATTER.

The Scouting experience of each boy is geared to his individual possibilities and needs. Scouting is a workable plan for associating boys of promise with men of character; together they become fellow discoverers. They learn skills and catch character traits from each other.

Scouting holds before the boy a code of ideals, not as mere lessons to be learned but as achievements to be carried through. Scouting teaches helpfulness through building the Good Turn habit, through practicing consideration for others, and through sharing and giving. Scouting recognizes the power of the far-reaching influence of the boy's own group, the patrol.

Scouting experiences build on outdoor living because of its appeal to the boy and also because outdoor life is a positive natural resource to help the boy grow stronger and more self-reliant.

Scouting strives to develop creative ability. It gives the

boy numerous chances to select and to make choices and to build an inner sense of adequacy.

Pay Attention to Boys

William S. Chambers was Scoutmaster of Troop 3, Springfield Methodist Church, Jacksonville, Florida, for over fifty years. More than 1,500 boys hiked and camped with him. A boy is always a challenge and a promise to him. He says, "The secret of helping a boy is to pay attention to him."

"The boy who says, 'Yes sir,' and No sir,' is pleasant to have around but not much of a challenge to me anymore. This boy already knows how to get along with people. He is already headed in the right direction. Of course we like that kind of boy, but the boys that are turned over to me by the juvenile court—boys who have serious problems with themselves and with other people—are the kind of kids that really keep me on my toes," he told me as he recalled his years of living with boys.

"We have a good troop committee. There are two or three of them present every Monday night," he explained. "We had one boy not long ago who was pretty disturbing at times—doing a good deal to upset our meetings. He was smart-alecky in his replies. He tried to make a joke of anything serious. He went so far that our minister got upset. One of the committeemen suggested that I tell the boy he was through.

" 'I've *never* told a boy that. Just ignore his shortcomings and have patience, and I'll talk to him,' I said. I sat down with the boy and said, 'I don't like the way you have been doing, but I still like *you*. I know that you have lots of possibilities. All this energy that you put into upsetting things—properly directed—could make you a real Scout. Now I am not going to okay another merit badge for you until you straighten up.'

"The boy looked me in the eye, and I kept looking right back at him. I wasn't angry—just firm. Pretty soon he smiled and said, 'OK, if that's the way it's going to be.' We shook hands, and he has been a different boy since then. That boy is now a patrol leader and is nearly an Eagle. That's the kind of boy that keeps me going."

The white-haired Scouter of years of happy leadership smiled as he thought back through the years to innumerable boys to whom he had "paid attention."

"A woman clerk in our office told me about a mischievous, bad boy that she had heard about. He had gone into a church and painted up and smeared the walls and had caused a lot of difficulty," Scoutmaster Chambers related. 'That is the first chapter of the story all right,' I told her, 'but do you know the second chapter?'

"Then I told her how that boy had come into my troop, had craved the respect and friendship of the boys and men in the troop, and had actually turned over a new leaf and now was one of our real leaders.

"It's been my experience that the boys who have caused me the most trouble have turned out later to be the most dependable leaders. Maybe that is because we paid more attention to them."

The Discipline of Earnest Purpose

People often talk about "discipline" as if it were a means of controlling people from without. They confuse discipline, which is "discipleship to a purpose," with a notion of restraint or force from outside—some sort of mental handcuffs or barrier—which discipline really is not.

Usually the person who has a driving purpose also has

strong discipline of himself. "Discipline," or teamwork, if you prefer to call it that, is most often lacking where people are being herded mechanically or managed arbitrarily by someone in authority over them, without their *understanding* or *caring about* the purposes and ends toward which they are being pushed and driven. Discipline is most often lacking when the person considers the group as a "they" group, a situation in which a person is being moved without knowing where he is going, why he should go, or the goal toward which he is being propelled.

When a person refers to the group as "we," this choice of words often is evidence of a genuine discipline over himself in the group situation. He sees purpose in his efforts.

When we have a driving purpose and a strong desire to help, we have achieved "discipline."

The Discipline of Goals

"He has a goal. He has an objective ahead." When we hear this said of a person, we usually find he is a disciplined person, a person under control—self-control.

He has a vision of a goal. He has an interest at stake. Since this is true, it would not be natural for him to be trifling, purposeless, idling in his approach to his task.

How Discipline Grows

"These boys need more discipline," the man said. We all agreed. "I'll give it to them!" the man said, and we waited, quite skeptical. The man put pressure on the group and attained a closer but forced control over the immediate situation, but discipleship to the cause did not result. The boys simply became more prudent in their purposelessness, but no boy became more disciplined, more intent on advancing the interest of the group.

How can we help discipline to grow? We can do this by helping the members of the group to see, to desire, and to work in harmony with the purposes of the group. They need to know why! They need to understand how. They need to develop discipleship to a cause.

Impertinent Punishment

If a boy's fault is one of wrong physical response, the correction may perhaps be made by physical means. But disobedience, carelessness, thoughtlessness are not primarily wrong physical responses. They are a failure of the boy's heart and mind to correlate and respond properly. Correction then should be directed at influencing these attitudes, changing the heart and mind *feelings*.

Spanking a boy in a horizontal position in a more or less sensitive region is not a direct approach to the desired result —does not lead even indirectly to influencing attitudes of heart. The approach is so roundabout that the boy will seldom make the correct interpretation of its significance. The contact is too far from the heart. Trouncing a boy because he is thoughtless and unappreciative is like being cranky with your wife because the weather is getting on your nerves. There is no logical connection between the cause and the result.

If punishment is to be effective, there must be an intelligent connection between the failure on the boy's part and the correction administered. The penalty must fit the wrong. The boy must see the significance of his error and the justice of the correction. The punishment must teach what we want it to teach, or else it is completely impertinent. To attempt to punish a boy for disobedience and thereby merely teach him dislike of the one administering the treatment is worse than no punishment.

The punishment needs to be understood by the boy and accepted as fair and fitting. He must understand its purpose. At least he must recognize down in his heart that it contains an element of justice—that he deserves it. Punishment is not an end in itself.

Getting Along with People

Getting along with people, all kinds of people, is a demanding skill—one not easy to acquire. We have to learn to live with people, even some who are pretty unreasonable at times. The boy learns on his paper route, in his Scout troop, in summer camp. Every hour of the day he learns to make adjustments. He develops skills in getting along with people. He learns that he can't always have his own way. He can't always be first.

We must not rob boys of values that come to them from squarely facing the disciplines of life. If boys don't learn how to meet some of these situations as they grow up, they will find themselves unprepared as young adults. They'll be baffled and sometimes broken by the sudden facing of the restraints and disciplines they should have learned to face gradually during their growing-up years.

There are dozens of disciplines that every boy must learn to face. Some people don't learn from experiences. They are merely soured by them. As parents and friends and leaders of youth, we must live close enough to youngsters to help them develop inner disciplines to face such situations.

Meeting Disappointments

There is a discipline that comes from learning to meet disappointments gracefully. You wouldn't want to shield and protect a boy from having occasional disappointments—even if you could—particularly the disappointments that come as a natural result of his own actions, would you? You don't want him to become a cynical, self-centered, complaining adult. Life is bound to have some disappointments, and even as a boy he needs to learn to take them in his stride.

Keeping in Touch with the Parents of Scouts

You will very seldom find a parent who is not genuinely interested in the enrichment of the life of his son. When you hear a Scout leader complain that parents are not interested in what the troop is doing, you may feel sure that either the troop is not succeeding in bringing into the boy's life any very significant influences, or if they are succeeding in this, somehow they are not effectively keeping in touch with parents, that the lines of communication between the troop and the parents of the boy are not what they should be.

Troop Scouters must not overlook the vital opportunity of keeping in touch with the parents of the boys whose lives they are trying to enrich. Certainly if leaders work separate and apart from parents, there will be many times when they work at cross-purpose though in their hearts their goals are the same.

Some troops have a family party once a year and feel then they have done their duty, but a once-a-year program is not enough. Some Scoutmasters invite the parents to a meeting now and then, and finding that the parents do not come in large numbers, they begin feeling sorry for themselves and say, "Oh, what's the use. I won't bother about the parents."

We need to draw parents into the troop, to give them different ways to share in the life of the troop. It is not always easy, but it is always *important*.

Three Fundamentals

"I have never seen a troop fail that kept plugging away at three fundamentals," Scoutmaster Sam said, "I can tell you in three words.

"The first word is *patrols*. Having patrols means that you have a *we* troop—a troop in which boys plan and dream and carry through. Patrols mean the difference between democracy and autocracy. Without patrols you have a regimented setup. With real patrols you have boy-guided action.

"The second word is *outdoors*. Troops don't die, they just starve to death from a lack of hikes and camping. Never do anything indoors that you can do outdoors.

"The third word is *advancement,* which of course means exploring new fields—growing, giving curiosity a chance to grow and work. I don't need to tell you about the fun of advancement when it is a real part of Scouting and not dehydrated, bookish, artificial drudgery."

Basic Values

"Why are they here? Most of them are here because of inadequacies in their boyhood days. Not five percent of them come from homes of criminality. But as boys they were not taught—or at least they did not learn—moral and citizenship responsibilities.

"There was something lacking in the training in their homes. If a boy doesn't learn certain basic values such as a sense of responsibility in his home, then he may possibly find such values in church, school, or community life. If he doesn't get them in any of these situations, I'm afraid he's pretty liable to make a mess out of his life."

(Warden Fred R. Dickson, San Quentin Prison, as interviewed by Walter MacPeek.)

Chapter 9

Making
Wise Choices

WHEN A BOY MAKES A CHOICE, HE IS PRAC-
TICING A FUNDAMENTAL HABIT OF GROWTH.
EVEN IF THE CHOICE SEEMS A SMALL ONE, IT
CAN LEAD TO MORE SIGNIFICANT CHOICES IN
DAYS AHEAD. CHOICES ARE CLOSELY RELATED
TO VALUES.

As the boy faces reality, as he develops skills of leading
and of following leaders, he gains self-confidence and awareness and develops courage and a sense of values.

Facing Reality—Assurance and Awareness

A boy needs to have a sense of assurance, a life philosophy
of understanding that this is a good world and that people
are generally decent and reasonably cooperative. He will succeed better if he is positive and constructive, expectant of
making his particular contribution in a somewhat reasonable
world.

Yet at the same time he needs to realize that everything
and everybody in the world will not be just as he would like
them to be. He is bound to have some rough going ahead of
him now and then. He needs to be prepared to meet some

people who are neither mature, nor well balanced, nor always entirely honorable in their way of dealing with others.

These are the sad facts of life, but they cannot very well be ignored. Now I would not suggest that we try to influence the young man to become a bitter pessimist. I do however suggest that a part of his growing up needs to include discovering that among the realities of the world around him there are such things as dishonesty and selfishness and inhumanity. These are realities, not mere theories.

This young man might very well prefer to live in a world where there is neither greed nor arrogance, no situations in which some men trample ruthlessly over others. He might very well dream of a world where there is no need to struggle against wrong and poverty and disease, but as a philosopher once said, "The essence of life is struggle." As a citizen he needs to recognize reality. He needs to *be prepared* to struggle.

I hope I am an idealist. I hope I see more good than bad when I look at things around me. But let's be clear-sighted idealists, seeing things realistically—not through rose-tinted glasses.

Experience—Plus Guidance

A boy's character is influenced as he goes through an experience. Adults cannot force him through an experience, but they can encourage and guide him.

"My policy is to let boys do what they want," one leader explained. A much wiser man replied, "I try to help boys to do what they want, but if through lack of wisdom or understanding they want to do something which is not wise, something which is unsocial, I try to give them guidance. If I did not do this I would not be worthy of being called a leader."

Carry-over

John sat at his typewriter, his parents' gift to him on his fourteenth birthday. It added immensely to his den.

"Oh, Johnnie! Will you go downstairs and look at the furnace for Mother?" came a voice from the living room.

"Yeah, Mother, just a minute."

One minute—two-three slipped by.

"Johnnie!"

"Yes, Mother, I'll go—"

The boy was busy writing an essay on "Mother." Out of the idealism of his boyish heart he was haltingly piecing together word upon word. More minutes slipped by, and his mother looked after the furnace herself.

"Why did you do it, Mother?" Johnnie asked. "You know that I'd do anything for you." The mother only smiled, and the boy went back to his den and his typewriter and his essay on "Mother."

Johnnie's mother began to think to herself when he showed her the article an hour later: "My boy is right in his heart. He means to be a good, dutiful citizen. How can his father and I help him to carry over the desires of his heart into action—into everyday living?"

The parents talked it over that night. They decided to be very careful lest they destroy the idealism itself. Perhaps through little everyday situations, plus encouragement, that characteristic of Johnnie's heart could grow into a habit of conduct.

A Chance Incident

"What was it that got you started thinking about the medical profession as your life work?" I asked a prominent Chicago surgeon not long ago.

"You'll be surprised when I tell you," he answered. "It was a compliment paid to a young waiter by an unknown guest at a restaurant."

Then as we sat looking out over that far-flung city so full of hope and challenge—and of misery—this saver of men's lives told me about his early boyhood. Nothing appealed to him very strongly as a possible vocation. He thought of many possibilities but somehow could not develop any enthusiasm for a special lifework.

Inasmuch as his family was in cramped circumstances, it had been arranged that he should do part-time service as a waiter in a little home-cooking restaurant around the corner from his dormitory room at the university.

"I had noticed a rather fine looking, neatly dressed, middle-aged man as he had come into and gone out of the restaurant on several occasions but had paid no particular attention to him. I don't think I ever knew his name," the doctor told me, reminiscing.

"One Sunday noon when I was dressed in my white jacket, he made this very chance remark as I was clearing away the dishes, 'Son, you begin to look like a doctor in those dark trousers and that brand-new white jacket.'

"Well that was about the only bit of vocational leadership I ever had. Somehow that compliment appealed to my pride. I was at an age when I wanted to look neat. The more I thought about it, the more I wondered why I had not thought of it before. I resolved to become a doctor!"

He sat looking across the city. Away in the distance was the smoke of the steel mill section. The water of the lake extended in a seemingly never ending expanse to the east. And this young doctor's fame has spread farther than either.

"I would probably have become a barber or a carpenter or might even have continued as a waiter if it hadn't been for that man. He'd be surprised if he knew. Well, as a result, I'm always pretty careful what I say to a boy. He can be mighty easily discouraged—or inspired."

Looking After Jim

Oh yes, though I'm a busy man,
I watch my boy, the best I can.
But I have so little time, you see.
So many groups depend on me.
I have so very little time
To keep an eye on my boy Jim.
I make him get to bed by ten,
Tell him who he mustn't play with, then
I buy his clothes with greatest care.
And my own barber cuts his hair.
Yes, though I'm a busy man
I look after him the best I can.

"But who looks *before* that boy of yours,
While you're so busy with your little chores?
Who looks *ahead* of your boy Jim
Who helps to build *his dreams with him?*
That's more of worth, I know, by far
Than merely looking *after* Jim.
Who watches campfire flames leap high?
Who helps plan challenge-tasks to try?
What of dream of home and hearth someday?
Who points *detours* along Life's way?
Who looks *ahead* along the trail with Jim?
While you're content with looking *after* him?

The Incentive Is Important

What a boy *does* is not always the important consideration. The incentive which moves him to action—the purpose in his heart—leaves the greatest residue in his character.

Often the needed inducement to right living is not so much an array of information as an impact of affection. We learn through our heart's yearning as well as through our brainpower.

It is more important that a boy be taught to love his country wisely than merely to know facts about it. Boys are impelled by admirations and hopes and dreams and dawning purposes. Ours is a task of setting up situations in which the boy's heart can be released into the task of right living.

Taking a Boy out of Scouting

Somehow I never could understand Scoutmaster Bill Johnson. He was a man of keen, discerning discrimination, and yet he used to say things in a blunt and often baffling way.

I remember one night when I was visiting his troop an irate mother appeared at the meeting and said to him, "I am going to take my boy out of Scouting!"

Entirely undisturbed and without batting an eye, Bill looked at her with a calmness that must have been irritating and said, "Your boy never has been *in* Scouting. He has merely been on the edge of it. It is true he has passed through a few requirements, but I'm afraid that he hasn't caught the least glimpse of what the spirit of a Scout ought to be."

As he talked further the woman's face registered one emotion after another. Finally when Bill was almost out of breath and the woman increasingly interested and indignant, she asked him, "Well, will you kindly tell me what this Scouting business is all about?"

Then Bill explained to her that Scouting was not just something that boys learn, not merely something that boys study to repeat back to the Scoutmaster. He explained to her that Scouting is a way of looking at life, a way of living, that it is an exploratory eagerness to face the problems of life; the Scouting attitude does not end with the expiration of a boy's Scouting membership. Very frankly and very bluntly he told her how difficult it had been to get across any vision of Scouting to her son, and told her that he was sorry that the opportunity to continue to try to influence her boy was now to be ended.

Two years later I heard that this boy was still in the troop and that he was earning merit badges and climbing toward the Eagle rank. I have never heard his name since that I have not wondered whether he has begun to get a vision of what Scouting is, for if he has, in the words of his fine Scoutmaster, "neither his mother nor anyone else in the world *can take him out* of Scouting."

Chapter 10

Reaching
High

A BOY NEEDS MANY KINDS OF ENCOURAGEMENT.
THAT ENCOURAGEMENT NEEDS TO CENTER
AROUND HIS IDEALS AND HIS SPIRIT—ESPECIALLY
SIGNIFICANT VALUES IN HIS EXPANDING LIFE.

The leader who commends and demonstrates wholesome conduct and high moral values helps boys reach high. No phase of a Scout leader's procedures can be of greater importance.

Influences in the Life of a Scout

The results of Scouting experiences are not accidental. A boy's world expands best under the guidance of purposeful adults. Take a program *shot through with purpose,* match the eagerness of boys with the devotion of earnest adults, and you can count on far-reaching results.

At every turn a boy makes choices. He reaches high for values. He helps plan. He shares. He learns to use judgment. He builds his personal citizenship standards through actual experience. He is an active part—a voting member of a democracy in action.

The atmosphere of hike and camp and meeting room has an important influence on him. He feels the impact of the spirit of the group. The Oath and Law and the Good Turn ideal challenge his very best. The ideals of Scouting grow on him; they become more compelling—more vital. He dreams. He takes part. He grows—in spirit and in skill. He prepares for his tomorrow.

Teamwork

You are only one man, and your hours are far too few. Get other men—devoted men—to help in what you do. Do not try to be a one man show. A wilted collar and a worried look too often lead a man to whine, to complain, and finally to quit.

Make this task a dream of many men, a dream in which you work with others like yourself. Make this a teamwork task.

Compass Points

No doubt you have often thought how very much a boy is gladdened by our interest in his world, our listening to his flowing talk.

He responds to thoughts we give as long as we do not press them, do not try to force or mold him to work according to *our* plan. We must leave him free to guide himself. A boy is eager when you come as an understanding friend to help discover, think through, and search with him, avoiding handing down as finished thought an act or plan that you have dreamed up.

As you explore with him, be sure you understand that while he is a boy, he is also more. He is one of a *group* of boys, a lengthened power growing out of his influence in his group.

He is a finger on a hand, and he moves with the others. If the hand moves one way, do not expect him to detach himself and move another way.

There are other thoughts we might explore—the magic of advancement, a force to motivate his inner growth, a sort of blueprint of a trail he will want to follow if we mark it well and garnish it with fun.

He feels the call of all outdoors challenging and calling forth his very best, the quest to cast off artificial things, his right to be himself, unhampered, uncluttered with things drab and crude. You can be a compass point to him.

High Purpose

It shall be my high purpose during the years ahead to do everything within my power to help the boy, our movement, and our nation to be and to become physically strong, mentally awake, and morally straight!

I will help strengthen and challenge boys—inspire and encourage them to forge ahead, eager to work in harmony with their God, eager to make their country a greater land.

"How is that different?" you may ask. "Different from last year and the year before, and the year before that?"

It is different in that we are going to try still harder. We are going to make Scouting influences more real and more challenging for many more thousands of boys. We will do our best to come to grips with conditions that influence youth. We mean business! *Action*—not empty words.

This is our goal, the earnest goal of our hearts and minds. Onward, not backward, not standing still—onward for God and country.

What America Has a Right to Expect of a Scout

The most important job for any boy is first of all to be a real boy. And being a real boy includes preparing now to be an able man.

Of course, America has a right to expect something worthwhile from every boy. Through schools supported by all and in numerous other ways America has invested—sometimes wasted—many hundreds of dollars on every boy. Naturally she has a right to expect something good from that investment. But America has a right to expect something even more from a boy who is a Scout. To a Scout we may say: Your parents and neighbors and people all around you are making investments in you by paying taxes, whether they want to or not. But the money which people invest in making Scouting experiences and values and influences possible for you they give in addition—because they want to—because they believe in you and your future. The citizens of America invest their dollars for you by maintaining your Scout council, camp property, training facilities for leaders, and other essentials to aid your troop in functioning in your behalf. Since these people invest in you, you are expected to make returns, not to them, but to America.

The most direct way you can make returns is by being a good citizen, a thoughtful, cooperative, helpful young citizen. The ideas of duty and responsibility may be old-fashioned ones, but they are still necessary in the life of the world. America has a right to expect you to begin now to be a thoughtful cooperative, helpful citizen. All your Scouting experiences are planned toward that end.

It is a matter of duty and responsibility, but at the same time you will have that feeling down inside that comes from knowing that you are doing right, and you will be proud and happy—and America will be strong.

A Better Lad If . . .

The four of us sat around the campfire talking. Walford was a wistful, quiet boy with a tendency toward pessimism. He had a good home background as far as I could observe. Like many highly imaginative people he was rather easily led— or misled.

"I don't know," he said to Joe—warmhearted, impetuous Joe Carney beside him, "I think that some people just have more of a chance. Their brains are bigger or something."

Joe did not agree. But he hesitated before replying, and hesitation was a rare quality for Joe.

Harold interrupted just as Joe started to speak. "I'll tell you what I think," strong emphasis on the "I"—"I think that some people are born good and others, well—not so good." There was a finality in his tone. As far as he was concerned it was settled for all time.

Dan Barstow had not said a word all evening. Dan was a slow-moving but understanding sort of fellow. He had a heart of gold and a pretty good head, too.

"Some people may naturally be better than others," he said slowly, "but I believe that any one of us can amount to a lot or a little, pretty much as we decide for ourselves. I saw a quotation over my boss's desk one day that read, 'The richest soil, if uncultivated, produces the rankest weeds.'"

We sat silent, but all of us were saying in our hearts, "I guess that's right."

And somehow a bit of Housman's verse kept coming back to me. As I closed my eyes, I murmured to myself:

There sleeps in Shrewsbury jail to-night,
Or wakes, as may betide,
A better lad, if things went right,
Than most that sleep outside.

The Real Test

The real test of a good Scout is whether he does his daily Good Turn quietly and without boasting. All the uniforms ever made, decorated with all the badges, do not make the wearer a Scout. Of course they may help as reminders to us.

A Good Turn is an *extra* kindness and service—something *more* than what courtesy and good manners require. Merely to answer a traveler's inquiry is not a Good Turn; it is natural courtesy. But to actually go with him is extending to him more courtesy than he has asked for, more than could be expected in the natural course of friendly good-neighborliness.

The Good Turn attitude and practice is the real test of a good Scout.

Quality of Leadership

Boys of promise are brought into contact with men of high purpose through Scouting experiences. When second-rate, mediocre men are in contact with boys of promise, the unfortunate result is often that the boys simply follow in their footsteps and become no better men themselves. Boys grow to be like the men with whom they live.

Jimmy's Zone of Influence

"Dad, how big do you suppose my zone of influences is?" Jimmy Waters asked at breakfast, his eyes fixed on the bowl of cereal before him.

James Waters, Sr., laid down his fork, looked at his thirteen-year-old son in amazement, and asked, "Your zone of what?"

Jimmy's face flushed. He heard his older brother laugh and say something about the "budding sociologist of the family."

"Oh, let it go—it doesn't matter anyway," Jimmy replied, busying himself with his breakfast.

Jimmy's feelings had been hurt. He had asked a serious question, and his father had looked at him as if he were out of his head, and his brother had laughed. The boy wished that they would forget all about it.

"But it does matter, son, we want to know. What was the expression—'zone of influence?'" Jimmy's father could be genuinely sympathetic at times.

Jimmy hesitated. "Yeah, that's what Mr. Mann said—'zone of influence.'"

"Might have known it would be something that Mr. Mann said. Kid, you're sure strong for your Scoutmaster. Good for you!" This came from his older brother.

"Jim, I can't quite figure out just what Mr. Mann may have meant. How did he use the phrase in talking to you?" The boy's father had exchanged a knowing glance with Mrs. Waters across the table. His question was couched in his most sympathetic and serious fatherly tone.

Jimmy, partially at ease again, explained: "Well, he told us that each of us has a zone of influence, a sort of territory in which people judge what happens by the kind of fellows we are. He said if we play the game the best we can and always do our level best, our zone of influence—those are just the words he used—would reach outside Harmonville, maybe to Chicago, maybe all over the country."

"Mr. Mann is a wonderful young leader. I'm glad he's your Scoutmaster, Jimmy," his mother said.

"Umm, well, I suppose your zone of influence, as Mr. Mann calls it, extends for a couple of blocks. Do you know just what he had in mind by 'playing the game'?" The boy's father was interested.

"Oh, just doing the best you can and giving everybody a fair break and not squealing when you get a bad break, not complaining. That's what he told us it means."

Jimmy's older brother was on his feet. "I've got to tear, or I'll be late to class. See you tonight." As he hurried down the street, the phrase, "zone of influence," somehow kept ringing in his ears.

A few minutes later as James Waters, Sr., started his car slowly down the street, he repeated half-aloud several phrases, "zone of influence—doing your level best—giving others a fair break—not squealing when you get a bad break—zone of influence."

And Jimmy on his way to school was turning over in his mind the question of something that he might do today to extend his zone of influence. It was pretty hard for a thirteen-year-old boy cooped up in school all day to do much about such things. Yet his Scoutmaster had said that no boy ever knew how far his power and influence might reach if he kept trying.

"Don't bother to write that letter, Miss Johnson. There is a change in that appointment." James Waters, Sr., watched as his secretary drew a long vertical line through shorthand hieroglyphics in her dictation book. "That will be all just now. Please ask Mr. Brown to step in."

"Did you wish to see me, sir?"

"Yes, sit down, Brown. How would you like to take charge of the Anderson Branch?" Mr. Waters watched the man's face light up.

"Would I like it? Of course I would. But I understood that—well—I had heard that another man was coming in for that." Brown made no attempt to hide the satisfaction he felt.

"Yes, we had almost decided to bring a man down from the Chicago branch. But we've been thinking how you've played the game here for all these years. You've been faithfully doing your best—constantly extending your zone of influence—and I feel it's only fair—just playing the game—to give you the chance that you've earned. You deserve the position."

The young lady at the typewriter was startled to hear her employer whistle. He didn't often whistle in the office. But James Waters, Sr., was happy today.

"No, fellows—even if you figure I'm chicken, or whatever you think, I'm not going to touch the stuff. It can't do me any good. It could do a lot of harm."

"Somehow drinking—even just sampling liquor—isn't playing the game with Mother and Dad and the school. Now go ahead and laugh and call me a cream puff, but I mean it"— and the gang knew Herbert Waters did mean it. But they didn't laugh. Instead they put glasses away sheepishly.

Herbert Waters threw back his shoulders as he walked, a happy spring in his step. He knew he was trying to play the game—he was doing his best. He was making himself count, extending his zone of influence.

An hour later, at the dinner table Jimmy's older brother tried to open the subject again in a blundering, big-brother way.

"Jimmy, have you thought any more about your 'zone of influence'? Honest, kid, I mean it." Jimmy was unconvinced. He flushed and was about to speak, but his father spoke first.

"Son," the older man remarked as he looked intently across the room, "you'll never really know how far your 'zone of influence' may reach if you keep playing the game—doing the best you can—always extending your zone of influence."

Scouting Ideals

It is no accident that as the result of his experiences in Cub Scouting, Boy Scouting, and Exploring—spread throughout the impressionable years from eight through seventeen—and as the boy moves toward a purposeful manhood, the growth of his character, citizenship, and fitness have been and are the earnest concerns of his parents and his Scout leaders.

Begin with him as a Cub Scout when, with all the natural solemnity of an eight-year-old, he promises to "do my best to do my duty to God and my country." Watch him as he is taught how to fold the flag. Note his boyish pride and loving care as he handles it.

Observe him a few years later as he stands tall and alert in his khaki uniform at Scout camp while the flag is being lowered. He is having everyday experiences here, too, in living as a good citizen, taking on more responsibility, showing concern for the needs of others.

More years go by, and this boy grown tall—now in high school—is an Explorer. He towers tall above his younger brothers as he considers the words of his Explorer Code. There is conviction in his voice as he says, "I will treasure my American heritage and will do all I can to preserve and enrich it."

Still more years pass, and this young American has become a man. He has profited from his Scouting experiences and from the influences of many men who have helped him. Now he has a job and a family and is making his influence count in his community. He is a citizen of a great country, and he understands, at least in part, his heritage from the founders of our country. He has grown to be a useful citizen.

Thus Scouting makes a difference in the life of a boy.

Everybody's Jamboree

You have no part, you say? You cannot go?
Yet, perhaps you *can* have a part.
It's everybody's Jamboree, a high event for all—
For Scouts who go and Scouts who stay at home as well—
For parents, brothers, sisters, friends.

Near forty thousand suntanned boys encamped in Idaho
And millions more—in spirit gay
Will gather at campfires with them there;
They'll sit 'long side as they swap treasures
And explore with friends the lore of many lands.

Millions of friends from every state
From every corner of our far-flung land—
Will read, and look and listen then,
Thrilled at Scouts in Jamboree.
No part? Not there?
Of course we'll have a part. We'll *all* be there!

Fellowship and comradeship and pageants huge
New depths of understanding and making of new friends—
Swapping and promoting knickknacks weird.
The hearts of all of us will reach out
Though we are far away.

Yes, though we stay home, each one of us is there—
By way of our ambassadors:
Lucky Scouts to number only many thousands.

Yet, not for them alone—
For all of us who feel a pride in them—
Our Jamboree unfolds—
To live forever on.

Cub Scouting Can Help to Build Home and Family Teamwork

Junior came rushing home from den meeting, shouting his enthusiasm so that all the neighbors could hear. He had been assigned the honor of leading the Pledge of Allegiance at the next Cub Scout pack meeting.

Such a situation may be pretty tough for Dad as he lays aside his paper, but *this* is a crisis. This boy wants to know *how*. It may have to wait till Father finishes the paragraph, but here is a youngster's desire for know-how at white heat!

As Dad works with him, he asks the boy some questions about the idea back of the flag. "Have quite a few people made sacrifices for us, for what the flag stands for?" he asks his son.

With his son, Dad looks up some background material in a reference book. Why do people fold the flag so that only the blue field shows? As Dad helps, the boy helps with his questions, his problems, and Dad is glad for the opportunity to work with his son. Through the kindly spirit of his helpfulness, Dad helps build deeper understanding and teamwork between himself and his son. What an opportunity for a father!

Work if you can in the spirit of a fellow discoverer. Your son will of course expect you to know all the answers, and you will know *some* of them. But do not be afraid to say, "Well, let's look that up. I'd like to know more about that too." It's a high compliment to say to a boy, "That's a *good* question. How can we find the answer to it?"

Surely being a fellow discoverer with your son is a more enjoyable as well as a higher parental vocation than being a mere question answerer. And, as a by-product, your son is gaining skill in searching for information from various sources.

"Why don't you ask Dad and Mother how you can help around the home?" the boy's handbook suggests. The wise father and mother will get well enough acquainted with the Cub Scout achievement program to see it as a common ground where son and parents often work together.

If you were to go to the pains to invent a series of helpful achievements for your son, you would probably devise a group of them not greatly different from those prepared for you in your son's Cub Scout book. These achievements are devised for you to use in helping your boy and your whole family develop the happy teamwork of doing things together.

Can other family morale-building situations grow out of Cub Scouting? Yes, dozens of them. Your attitude toward your boy's den and toward his Den Mother and Den Chief can be far-reaching. It is not a bad idea to observe, within your Cub Scout son's hearing, once in a while, "Mrs. Hubbard certainly does a nice job as a Den Mother; you're fortunate to be in Den 4," or "I'm glad Clayton is your Den Chief—he's a good friend to have."

While you are being a booster for your son's den, Father, don't be satisfied to keep your relationship on a merely *verbal* basis. How about offering to take the den—your boy and his pals—on a trip to the zoo, or to the museum some Saturday afternoon, or on a trip to take photographs or to gather walnuts—or on a work session down into your workshop?

It is a pretty good idea, too, for Mother to offer to help with an occasional den meeting or to be willing to take over if the Den Mother has to be out of town. After all, a den is a cooperative project directed by the parents of the boys in the den. Everybody helps, and everybody benefits!

Another way that parents can help build a strong family unity is through their relation to the Cub Scout pack and its monthly pack meetings for parents and boys. Whenever the question is raised concerning your taking part, a positive approach helps a lot.

"Why of course we'll take part in our pack meeting! We will go because we enjoy being there. We want to see the other dens and we are proud of own den in action. It's the very least that we can do to support the chairman, the Cubmaster, and the Den Mothers for all that they are putting into our pack." By wholehearted cooperation in Cub Scouting activities you are building a high sense of *family unity and pride.* You are helping your boy become a participating citizen, ever ready to do his share for the common good. Granted that you can have pride in family and happy home relationships without Cub Scouting, certainly you are surer of achieving it to a high degree by using the added opportunities that Cub Scouting opens to you.

Jamboree at Valley Forge

I wonder what they'll see, these boys who will come from every part of our land—who will gather here in a friendly Jamboree at Valley Forge.

Of course, they will see some Scouts of other lands. They will gain a better grasp of their common world with all its heartaches, hopes, and dreams. They will see the ocean and tall mountain peaks and broad green spreads of farms and homes. They will see the progress of our present day, and some will vision days long past. Some will glimpse in campfire light the pioneers who came from other lands, who built and left for us a heritage of hope. Some will vision lives for others lived, days of struggling against frontier odds, yet homes and schools and cities built. They will give thanks for all who have gone before, for those who have built for us a world to take pride in and to love.

But most of all I think these boys gathered in their Jamboree at Valley Forge will dream ahead. They will pledge to do their best to help make tomorrow's world far better still for all who follow them.

Qualities of an Explorer Advisor

I looked across the desk at the old-timer. His thinning hair was almost white, yet little lines around his eyes gave the impression that somehow he got a lot of fun out of life. For forty years he had been a part of Scouting. Thousands of young men had grown to manhood under his encouraging guidance.

"Tell me," I requested, "what makes Exploring really tick?"

"That's an easy one," he answered smiling, "a good Explorer Advisor."

"Then tell me what are the qualities of this good Explorer Advisor? Why does one man really get across while another one may not?"

"A man who deals with young men of Explorer age has to be able to think fast. He has to have had the experiences that these boys are seeking; he must see values in them. He has to remember how he felt when he was a young man of Explorer age."

"Well, then you would say that he has to be a very understanding man."

"That's right, very understanding, and he must have a deep respect for an Explorer-age boy. He must not try to decide for these young men. He must respect the Explorers so highly that he gives them every opportunity to decide for themselves. He must have a good deal of 'us' and 'you' in his thinking rather than 'I' and 'me.'"

The old-timer looked out the window for a moment across the green hills. "The Explorer Advisor has to have the ability to make fellows feel comfortable when they come to him to talk things over."

We talked on about the qualities of an Explorer Advisor, and the old-timer made this observation, "Boys of this age often can't tell you what they want. Sometimes they feel pretty frustrated. If they have an Explorer Advisor whom they have confidence in, whom they can accept as a friend and as a coach, who makes suggestions to them as a fellow citizen, they are pretty liable to go along with him."

I asked about special interests and skills that an Explorer Advisor might have.

"The ideal Explorer Advisor is primarily interested in the growth of young men. Most of the outstanding advisors I know are fathers and are much more interested in the development of young men than they are in special techniques. They recognize skills as important—as a means to Explorers' becoming able, well-adjusted men."

Just What Must We Prepare Him For?

Scouting is an experience in controlled living. A strong Scout troop brings its members face-to-face with many interesting experiences. These Scouting experiences help a boy to meet life.

"I never meet a man," one Scoutmaster recently told me,

"that I don't say to myself, 'Perhaps he was a Scout once,' and too often I have to continue, 'If he was, his troop failed to prepare him fully for life. Perhaps his troop was a sort of stunt parade rather than a force that coordinated all the forces of his life into a united front.'"

Experience in a Scout troop should teach a Scout how to evaluate people.

Scouting should teach a boy that important ability of self-leadership. A boy who experiences the richest possible Scouting should build a reserve power, a control over himself. Scouting experiences, properly guided, should help a boy develop the power to plan, to organize, to be orderly.

The most discriminating Scout leader I ever knew once told me, "I learn most about my boys by watching their reactions to experiences. It is not what comes into their life alone that counts most. A boy's reactions to things count most."

Where does the power of "determination" come from? How does a boy achieve it? How can we as Scout leaders help Scouts develop "selectivity"? If we are to make a vital contribution to their lives, we must help boys develop that ability to select, to choose, to pick the best from the vast array of life's possibilities that comes before them daily.

When you are debating whether or not you will suggest a certain program or project to boys, ask yourself this one question and decide on that basis: "What will be the effect on the boys?"

I Listen to Boys

"We have full confidence in our Scoutmaster; I guess it is partly because he has confidence in us and shows it. He is quick to see our point of view, and he never ridicules or attempts to embarrass anyone in any way. I have a feeling my

Scoutmaster expects me to be successful in whatever I undertake. It is his confidence in my ability that encourages me to work for higher ranks. He seems to be interested in me and gives me the feeling that he is my friend, ready and anxious to help," a Scout told me in an interview.

"My Scoutmaster is good-natured enough to be likeable, but hard-boiled enough to protect his own rights and the rights of others. He has no pets and draws no favoritism," another said.

"Our Scoutmaster is very thorough in whatever he does and expects us to do our work carefully and well. Sometimes he preaches about "excellence," but we like him so much that we are willing to accept even the preaching. You know, the more I think about it, this business of excellence is pretty important, particularly if a fellow is going to be a doctor or a builder or something like that where a great deal depends on him."

"My Scoutmaster can see my point of view as well as his own," another Scout explained, "He can make things really interesting and encourage you to want to find out about things. Sometimes he seems more like one of the boys than a grown-up. He is more interested in developing us into people than he is in trying to cram a lot of information into us. I like that."

"Our Scoutmaster has a sort of quiet air about him that shows plainly that he expects obedience. I have never seen him lose his temper or be out of patience with anyone," another Scout explained. "I talk to him as a close friend and pal, and anything I tell him is kept in confidence. He is fair with me."

"Our Scoutmaster is never cross or loud in order to make us behave," was another comment. "He is firm and just, and we naturally try to measure up to what he expects of us. Somehow what he wants us to do is always important and interesting, and we realize the value of getting his help. He has a lot of patience."

"If you make a mistake," another Scout said, our Scoutmaster helps you to see how you can correct it. At the same time, he doesn't make you feel ashamed. He does make you want to try harder. I owe a lot to him."

The final comment left me thinking, for the boy said. "My Scoutmaster understands a good deal about human nature, especially in its weak places."

Keynote of Boyhood

"What are the characteristics of youth?" the visitor asked the Scoutmaster.

"Let's watch and see what we can discover," he suggested, pointing to three boys near the clearing of the woods.

The man looked. He saw a boy with cheeks puffed out trying to play a bugle. He saw another boy pointing and jumping up and down, much excited and greatly amused over his friend's bad bugling techniques. And the third boy, camera in hand, was taking a picture of the two.

"They're all doing the same thing," the Scoutmaster observed.

"How can you say that? One is trying to bugle; another is doing open-air gymnastics, and the other is taking a picture."

"*Action*—that's the keynote of youth. They are all in action, all expressing themselves. It doesn't make much difference whether it's bugle or camera or just jumping—they all speak the language of boyland—motion."

Expression, action—they are the keynote of boyhood.

Index